Home on the Plains

Quilts and the Sod House Experience

NEBRASKA STATE HISTORICAL SOCIETY RG 2608.PHI100

Home on the Plains:
Quilts and the Sod House Experience
Kathleen L. Moore
Stephanie Grace Whitson

Editor: Edie McGinnis
Designer: Amy Robertson
Photography: Aaron T. Leimkuehler
Illustration: Eric Sears
Technical Editor: Jane Miller
Production Assistance: Jo Ann Groves

Published by:
Kansas City Star Books
1729 Grand Blvd.
Kansas City, Missouri, USA 64108

First edition, first printing
ISBN: 978-1-935362-80-7

Library of Congress Control Number: 2011920058

Printed in the United States of America
by Walsworth Publishing Co., Marceline, MO

To order copies, call StarInfo at (816) 234-4636
and say "Books."

Contents

Foreword 6

PART ONE: ARRIVING 8
  Susan Ophelia Carter Payne 12
  Luna Elizabeth Sanford Kellie 15
  Maria Jane Forsythe Newton 18

PART TWO: SETTLING IN 22
  Grace McCance Synder 26
  Rachel Rice Newton 28

PART THREE: STAYING ON 30
  Grace Susannah Budd Wood 38
  Manerva McWilliams Hersh
    & Margaret Alice Osborne Raney 42

PART FOUR: QUILT PROJECTS 44
  Ward Family Nine Patch Doll Quilt 46
  Heimer Family Snowball Quilt 50
  Newton Family "Laws O Massey" Quilt 56
  Sageser Family Pomegranate Quilt 60
  Sageser Family Pot of Tulips Quilt 68
  Wood Family Wedge and Circle Quilt 76
  Comer Family Botch Handle Quilt 82
  Hersh Family Double Nine Patch Quilt 88

Endnotes 93
Acknowledgements 95
About the Authors 96

Foreword

"I was born in a sod house."

It was 1976 and the man who uttered those words was my Lincoln, Nebraska, next-door neighbor. I can still see Mr. K. standing on his back patio practicing his golf swing (he paid my two children a nickel for returning any golf-ball sized "wiffle balls" they found in our flower beds). He loved golf and his wife and worried every year lest the peonies not bloom in time for Decoration Day. In spite of my obvious fascination with the idea of a sod house, Frank didn't want to talk about it other than to say he sincerely hoped "the old pile of dirt" had fallen in. So much for my romantic notions of interviewing a "real pioneer." But the spark was lit.

Mr. K. passed on and we moved away, eventually settling on an acreage in Otoe County, Nebraska. Nebraska history took on new meaning as we walked through an abandoned pioneer cemetery nearby, discovering that the five graves along the road were siblings. *How did their mother survive that,* I wondered, looking at my four children—three of whom would have died of childhood illnesses in the 1800s. (Thank God for that gooey pink medicine.) Perched beneath a pine tree, I surveyed tombstones and mounds of earth long-since unmarked when their wooden markers rotted away, asking questions of my home-schooled children. *Was there a doctor nearby? How far did they walk to school? How many of these trees were here when these children played up the road?* We sought answers as part of our Nebraska history unit, and, once again, I was drawn to the stories of western women, especially the ones who lived in soddies.

When, in 2001, I co-curated a quilt exhibit with the International Quilt Study Center and Museum and the Nebraska History Museum, reading donor files was part of the selection process. The phrase "came west in a covered wagon … used in a sod house … " recurred, and once again the lives of women inhabiting sod houses beckoned.

Kathy Moore was drawn to the potential for a new approach to uncovering evidence of women's experiences during the era of plains settlement, a subject about which she was eager to learn more. An idea became a project. Ours was a partnership of mutual interest and enthusiasm and over the next five-plus years we searched for other quilts … and found some. We sought stories … and we found some. The result is this lovely book about some of our pioneering predecessors and the quilts they were inspired to make.

As twenty-first century women, we've learned a lot from our collective foremothers. The thing that amazes us most about them is that they took time for beauty. They cut scalloped edges on window shades and shelf paper. They filled their broad windowsills with geraniums and roses. And they pieced quilts. Had keeping a family warm been the sole reason for quilt making, it would have been much simpler and certainly more efficient, and time-wise, to whack off a length of fabric and make and tie a comforter. But somewhere in between baking and birthing and mending and making shirts and planting gardens and working in the fields alongside husbands and nursing children and battling bedbugs and fleas, these women spent hours cutting cloth into pieces and stitching those pieces back together in intricate patterns. To those who have never fed their souls with creativity, it might seem madness. Others are more likely to call it a cure for—or at least momentary relief from—the crushing weight of endless labor in a mostly hostile environment.

Whatever your personal beliefs about the role of creativity, it is our sincere hope that these quilts, known to have shared a sod house woman's life, will cross time and fulfill the hope our foremothers sometimes inscribed on their quilts: "Remember me."

Kathleen L. Moore and Stephanie Grace Whitson
Lincoln, Nebraska
2011

PART ONE

Arriving

"Some would say Eva how can you leave all your people and go away to Nebraska its so far away. I told them I do hate to leave my dear mother sister and brother but I am going with my husband and we are going to get us a home of our own. Where we can be to ourselves. And that meant so much to us."[1]

NEBRASKA STATE HISTORICAL SOCIETY RG2608.PH2938

Maude and May Tuck and family passing through Nebraska's South Loup Valley in 1891-92 on their way to Montana. The Tuck children, Leona and Ira, were asleep in the wagon. Note the comforters and other quilts hanging from the wagon bows.

"People, like cabbages," Irish immigrant W.H. Taylor once said, "improve by transplanting."[2] Taylor had landed in Canada with his family at the age of four, left for New York at sixteen, worked his way west to Leavenworth, Kansas, with a plan to drive mules across the plains to Salt Lake, and ended up in Exeter, Nebraska. His enthusiasm notwithstanding, a young man in good health striking out on his own is a far different undertaking than a couple with children leaving an established home and extended family to head west. Why did they do it? What was it like?

In her "Memories of Pioneer Days," Eva Klepper recounts months of hard work as she and her mother-in-law prepared to emigrate from Tennessee to Nebraska in 1879. Together, the women harvested and canned or dried currants, gooseberries, cherries, peaches and "all the fruit we could, as there were no fruit trees in Furnas County." They "sold all the furniture," and "packed ... pictures, dishes, and glassware among the bedding to keep it from breaking. We loaded our wagon ... put in trunks, boxes of fruit, a chest with some clothing, bedding and pillows that we would need to sleep on."[3]

Eva's family and thousands like them migrated west in the shadow of Oregon and California-bound pioneers who'd crossed Nebraska via the Oregon and Mormon Trails. For those earlier travelers, Nebraska was little more than a vast expanse of worthless property standing between them and their destination. Early maps labeled it the "Great American Desert." In the latter half of the nineteenth century, though, political, social, and economic changes transformed Nebraska from obstacle to destination.

HO FOR ... NEBRASKA!

The 1862 Homestead Act signed by President Abraham Lincoln wasn't the first legislation encouraging homesteading. It was, however, unique because the land was virtually free to heads of households who could certify improvements and five years of permanent residence.[4]

History has demonstrated that five years of permanent residence in Nebraska was anything but easy. Still, among Civil War soldiers dissatisfied with postwar "quiet life," with the South in a shambles, after financial panics in 1857 and 1873, and because of the economic depression in the 1870s, many saw this Homestead Act as the answer to a once impossible dream: individual property ownership. By 1870, nearly two million acres had been claimed in Nebraska.[5]

Ina Abrahamzon's family emigrated from Texas to North Loup, Nebraska, hoping to improve her father's health. After a month-long wagon trek north, the family lived with their friends until they located their own homestead.

Louisa Wilhelmina Lange came as a result of romance. As a newlywed, and despite her fiancé's promises to the contrary, Louisa began housekeeping in "the crudest type of western home—the dug-out." Her sod house was soon completed, however, and "enhanced with muslin-covered walls and gunny-sack floor over a padding of straw."[6]

Economic and political conditions in Europe also drew thousands to Nebraska. When serf labor in Bohemia ended, so did John Ziska's position as overseer on a baron's estate. Disappointing results from farming in Wisconsin and coal mining in Missouri led them on to Nebraska and, in the spring of 1869, they rented a dugout in Fillmore County.

The William McGhies of Aberdeen, Scotland, decided to try their fortune in America after reading letters published in the Aberdeen Free Press. Convinced that America was a land of opportunity, the McGhies and their four children set sail for America, and Mr. McGhie bought railroad land about three miles south of Exeter, Nebraska. When the family's early experiences were not very encouraging, McGhie said, "we'll just bundle up what we hae and gae back to Scotland," but his wife refused. "Na, we're ance here and we're nae to gae back."[7]

HO FOR NEBRASKA BY WAGON

Emily Plummer had already moved several times before climbing aboard her Nebraska-bound wagon in 1872: from New Hampshire to Massachusetts and then to Wisconsin where she married E.W. Carpenter. While their specific reasons for setting out for Nebraska are not mentioned in Emily's diary, her account of the thirty-eight-day covered wagon journey west provides fascinating insights into the realities of trail life for a future Nebraska homemaker.

August 12	We started for Nebraska. Took dinner on the Yarrington place. There father said goodbye. Camped at night by Dutch Jake's.
August 17	342 cattle herded
August 18	I did some washing. We had plenty of mosquitoes (she mentions mosquitoes often)
August 19	Crossed the line at noon (referring to the crossing into Iowa. Mrs. Carpenter often mentions things like "water but no feed for cattle," or "feed but no water.")
August 20	Huldah sick and I care nothing about cattle.
August 22	Took dinner two miles east of Belmont … had blacksmithing done.
August 23-24	Had minute pudding. Camped 7 miles east of Eagle Grove. Had a thunder storm and at day light is still raining. All got wet but the babies. Met a family going back to Worth Co. Iowa. Camped at 2 O'clock. Washed and dried the bedding and rested the oxen. Hot day—the warmest we have had. Plenty of mosquitoes.
August 30	John shot a chicken. Took dinner on the prairie.
August 30	Fried cakes and coffee for breakfast.
August 31	Took dinner on a small raise. Had corn. At night west of Dennison. Bought apples and crackers.
September 2	It rains. We keep close to the wagons. Went through Dunlap at noon. Camped on a vacant lot close to the river. Washed and done some mending.
September 4	A cool day. Hope to see the Missouri.
September 19	We arrived at Gibbon.[8]

HO FOR NEBRASKA BY RAIL

The same year he signed the Homestead Act, President Lincoln also signed the Pacific Railway Act into law. This legislation called for the construction of a transcontinental railroad from the Atlantic to the Pacific oceans. In 1864, a second act "sweetened the pot" by granting the railroad "ten square miles (per mile of track laid) in a checkerboard pattern on both sides of a free right-of-way."[9] The potential revenue from selling that land to homesteaders, along with government loans ($16,000 per mile of track laid across the plains) and private investment accomplished the desired result.

The transcontinental railroad was completed in 1869, and railroads launched a massive advertising campaign to draw immigrants to Nebraska. Pamphlets touted cheap land and liberal terms. Published in German, Czech, and other languages, and distributed at major ports in the Eastern U.S. and Europe, the pamphlets got results—as did reduced fares, free lodging in "immigrant houses," and free seed.[10]

The only information known about this family is the photographer's note which reads, "starting a new family Northwest of West Union, Nebraska, 1866." Note the Jenny Lind bed just inside the door.

Railroad propaganda her mother read in 1871 resulted in Luna Sanford Kellie's emigration. According to Luna's reminiscences, Martha Lois Sanford repeatedly urged her husband to go west and "get in on the ground floor."[11] When Martha died in 1873, her husband traveled alone to file on both a homestead and a timber claim. James then wrote encouraging his married daughter, Luna, and her husband, J.T., to come west and "get hold of some more land." Luna came first to keep house for her father and brothers until J.T. could join them. Eventually, the Kellies built their own home, joining the ranks of thousands of families setting up housekeeping in homes constructed from prairie sod.

Susan Ophelia (Carter) Payne

*"made a waist to my wedding dress,
also 2 sheets, 2 ticks and 1 pair of pillow cases
and sewed up two pair more that I didn't hem."[12]*

S usan Ophelia Carter was born in Grundy County, Illinois, in July of 1860 to Lewis Wood and Rachel (Wheeler) Carter. Like many other immigrants to the American west, Susan's family moved in fits and starts, often with family groups and friends. In July, 1886, Susan would have been 26 years old, well past marriageable age. That year she taught school in Valley County, in south-central Nebraska, possibly in a sod building.[13] That Christmas she received a small red leather-bound diary from a friend and it was in this little red book that Susan faithfully recorded her daily tasks and experiences.

During the school year Susan boarded with several families in the community, some of whom were long-standing family acquaintances. She had a beau, Will Payne, with whom she apparently had an understanding about their future as husband and wife.

Will headed west in February of 1887, along with friends and family members, to homestead in Box Butte County, Nebraska. Susan stayed behind to finish teaching out the semester and prepare to move west. She spent her spare time in the following months writing in her diary and sewing for herself and others in the community.

NEBRASKA STATE HISTORICAL SOCIETY RG0846.AM

Frontispiece of diary given to "Susie Carter," Christmas of 1886. Susie came to Nebraska as a child with her family.

Susan mentions making shirts for men in the family and community. On March 5, 1887, she made her first "comfortable" which she intended to send to Will. In the nineteenth century "comfortables" or "comforts" were "soft, thick quilts, used as substitutes for blankets, and laid under the bedspread. One of them is equal in warmth to three heavy blankets: and they are excellent in cold winters for persons who like to sleep extremely warm."[14] Thick batts or older quilts could be enclosed in pieced or whole-cloth slipcovers and then randomly tied to secure the batting.

On March 14, her diary reads, "sewed up my calico dress at noon. Sewing on my under clothes this evening." And on March 19, she noted, " … done lots of sewing today." By March 22, she " … got my sewing done nearly. Don't know what I'll do all the week."

On April 7, Susan got to do some sewing on a machine belonging to Mrs. T.C. Hennolds. The practice of sewing on a machine belonging to someone else was common, especially in small and rural communities, in the decades leading up to the turn of the century. Sewing machines were commercially available before the Civil War, but they were expensive enough that often only one or two women in a given community would have one and they would make it available for others to sew on. It wasn't until after the Civil War that sewing machines became affordable, frequently on time payment plans made available by the Singer Company. By the 1870s and 1880s these machines were much more typical as household appliances and were often featured as prized possessions in Solomon Butcher's pictures of prairie households.

On April 9, Susan added to her hope chest. She " … made a waist to my wedding dress, also 2 sheets, 2 ticks and 1 pair of pillow cases and sewed up two pair more that I didn't hem." Two days later she " … cut out her percale dress … " On the 15th she " … sewed on my white dress and wrote a letter to Will." Most interestingly, on April 30, Susan mentions that a "Mrs. McIntyre came down and helped me tie my comforter that Ma sent me."

By May 13, school was over and Susan headed for Box Butte County with friends Mamie Preston and Cella Redlon. They rode the train part of the way west then traveled by wagon and horseback. On what must have been a thrilling adventure, Susan caught up with Will on May 20 and two days later he took her to see the claim. She thought it was "just grand." A few days later she was alone on the claim and planning a garden patch. On the 29th she wrote, "Will came out and took dinner with me on the claim. I have no table yet and we ate off from the bed. Great times at our little old sod shanty on the claim." The next day she "fixed up one suit for Will." What followed were days of planting seeds in gopher holes, making shirts

for Will, and occasionally sharing dinner with him in their little sod shanty.

In late June, Susan traveled to the small nearby town of Nonpariel to "get up a class in embroidery." Her diary then lists numerous sewing assignments she assumed for local clients. Interspersed between these assignments are domestic duties like cooking and laundry and mention of details related to the construction and repair of her sod house. She also was prone to severe headaches which lasted for days during which Will walked out to the claim where he would do her laundry and cook for her.

Other times Susan's notes prove she was capable of providing for herself when the need arose. In September when she was alone on the prairie and feeling poorly, she went out with her small rifle and " … shot 5 little birds

> *Will came out and took dinner with me on the claim. I have no table yet and we ate off from the bed. Great times at our little old sod shanty on the claim.*

to make broth of." With an element of pride she noted, "I shot them all in the head."

Finally, on October 29, the newly arrived minister, Elder Collins, appeared at the doorway of her soddy at supper time and declared that she and Will "would be married this eve." While one may wonder what they had been waiting for, it is clear there was no ordained minister available to perform the ceremony until the Reverend Collins came to town. According to Susan's notes, without further adieu, that evening he performed their marriage ceremony "in their little sod shanty on the claim."

During the span of 1886-1887, Susan spent a lot of time sewing for herself and others, much of it while she was alone on the prairie in Box Butte County, Nebraska. The December following her wedding Susan earned fifty cents for cutting and fitting a dress for her friend, Jennie Collins.

While there are no explicit descriptions of quilt making from this one-year diary, there are references to finishing "comfortables" and to the sewing Susan was doing for herself and others. Her words give us documentary evidence of the kinds of stitching a skilled and resourceful woman on the plains would have been doing. She made everything from her underclothes to dresses for herself and other women and shirts for men as well as a suit of clothes for her fiancé, Will. It is clear that she made at least one "comfort" and she received one from her mother to finish with the help of a friend.

Susan and Will remained in the little community of Nonpareil, in Box Butte County, for about three years after which they seem to have moved around within and between nearby states.[15] In 1910, Will and Susan had been married 22 years and Susan had borne two children. Their son, Ansel, born in 1888, died when he was 12 years old. A second son, born in 1891, died ten days later.[16] They adopted a daughter, Marguerite L. Payne, who survived to adulthood.

Will died of complications from asthma in 1914 in Morrill, Nebraska, where they had lived for the previous six or seven years.[17] Susan moved to Torrington, Wyoming, for a brief while. In 1915 she remarried and lived, first in Kansas, then Colorado where she died in May, 1946, at the age of 85 years.

Susan's life was probably fairly similar to that of her contemporaries. Theirs was a continuum of hard and physical work, interspersed by the adventures of a pioneering life. In between, many women on the plains managed to indulge their need to create decorative, yet utilitarian, textiles. Some of those textiles, quilts in particular, can be seen in the pictures Solomon Butcher took as he crossed Nebraska recording the sod house experience before the march of time and modernization erased the evidence of their experiences.

Luna Sanford Kellie

"I hurried myself to finish a fine quilt I had about ⅓ made before marriage. . ."[18]

NEBRASKA STATE HISTORICAL SOCIETY RG3914.PH3

Luna Sanford Kellie and her five-month-old baby boy arrived in Nebraska in 1876. Luna was to keep house for her father and brothers while awaiting the arrival of her husband, J.T. Luna's first impression of sod house homemaking was far from positive. "I thought a sod house would be kind of nice, but the sight of the first one sickened me." She had expected it to be "nice and green and grassy … not such a dirty looking thing." The day her husband arrived later that year, was "the happiest day of my life … we were together again and resolved come weal or woe nothing should ever part us again. We were young and full of hope and nothing could daunt us."

When their own soddy was ready for the young family, they purchased "a No. 7 cook stove, a ½ gallon jug full of vinegar and a gallon jug full of molasses, a sack of flour, sugar, tea, coffee, salt and pepper, a hoe and a rake" for their home. J.T. made a high chair and a bureau from packing boxes, built a table and bedstead, and made stools by "sawing the tops from logs."

Luna's reaction to moving into her "half finished sod house with straw roof" stands out in great contrast to her opinion of her father's dugout. " … hanging an extra quilt and some sheets around on the sod walls made them seem

Luna Kellie came to Nebraska as a young mother, arriving via train with toddler in tow.

homelike … behold we had a home and no rent to pay, who could ask for more … We always planned for a large family … we thought twelve the least number that would do us and fifteen would be better." (She would have thirteen.)

Luna's reminiscences illuminate the life of a woman who was a true partner in every aspect of homesteading. "He started breaking for sod corn … and I would go around dropping three kernels about three feet apart." She helped put up hay. "Willie would stay on the ground with his Pa and I would load and then we take the load home sometimes a mile or two … and I would stack while J.T. pitched it off." She was nine months pregnant when she "started in to help J.T. cut the broom corn but we only worked two or three days when I got sick in the night. J.T. made a hurried run a mile east for a neighbor woman who hurried back and about daylight Friday we had another lovely little boy whom we named at once after his father … I got dinner on Monday and then being so worried about the broom corn went out and helped cut some … Tuesday morning I wrapped the new baby in a quilt and took it to the field and worked all day … I did not get real strong for a long time."

When a pregnancy prevented her driving the harvester and her husband had to hire a substitute, she found another way to help: "I remember he (the hired man) needed some work shirts and sent and bought some shirting and I made him two all by hand back stitched all the seams and felled them and charged him 25 cents each and I was proud to think that I could help that much … "

Four days after Luna's third baby, Susie, was born in August of 1879, she was up cooking for the threshing crew. She "cooked up a jar full of sauce made six or eight pies and three or four cakes and baked a whole boiler full of bread … a lot of beef to boil and a large roast. We had abundance of vegetables sweet and Irish potatoes, cabbage, carrots, onions, tomatoes, squash etc. … "

SPEAKING OF STITCHING:

"I realized I must make over some of my clothes I had before marriage nice white skirts etc. into baby clothes as there was no prospect of getting anything new but I had no white thread … We paid 5 cents a spool in Rockford and I thought it would be probably 6 here but as a neighbor was going to town I gave him my 7 cents to get a spool of white thread. Imagine my disappointment when he … said he could not get the thread as it was 10 cents. So I started sewing the nice white goods by hand with black thread."

"I took my first trip to town about eighteen months after I came and got outing flannel and flannel for under clothes for us all … "

The winter of 1880-1881 was "a very long and cold winter … set in early and had lots of snow. … J.T. had bought me a new Singer Machine and I made good use of it making all the clothes we all wore. I had done this before by hand only occasionally taking some long seams down to sew on Mrs. Strohl's machine. Machines were not so high then I think we paid thirty or thirty-five dollars for it."

She traded butter for fabric and held out for the best possible trade. "I went with them with my 2 jars of butter … they would pay only ten cents a pound … and when I priced their flannel it was eighteen cents a yard for the same quality as was fifteen at Kenesaw. So I took my butter back home to take to Kenesaw."

Luna took pride in making shirts for her husband. "I was mighty proud of him and have never seen before or since such a handsome man. He had always worn white shirts as bridge foreman and I could not bear to see him in any others in the summer so always made them of unbleached muslin with liner cuffs and collars and the gray trousers I made as Grandma Smith who had learned the tailor trade taught me and they always fit so nice and he … did not wear overalls for years … The cloth only cost ten cents a yard and I traded eggs for it and always got several at a time so he could look nice … for winter he had dark blue flannel shirts which were warm and looked nice too."

LUNA'S SOD HOUSE QUILT STORIES:

Soon after Luna arrived in Nebraska, a neighbor woman's daughter came to stay while her father and brothers were away harvesting for neighbors. "We had nothing to do except cook a little for ourselves so I hurried myself to finish a fine quilt I had about one-third made before marriage. It was a log cabin of fine materials and I had abundance of pieces for at least two quilts." Luna's company offered to finish a quilt for her in return for enough pieces to make herself a wedding quilt. Luna never received her quilt. The "friend" eventually brought her first child to church "wrapped in a small quilt I knew I had pieced myself … at last I went to the house for them. There was the baby quilt soiled and pretty well worn, two or three chair cushions also worn, and shirts made from the larger pieces … all she seemed to find was a small handful of pieces for me."

"One of the last of the trips I made to Kenesaw with wheat was against a very strong north wind. I had a very heavy comforter … on the seat and over the back … just as we turned the corner … the wind … turned the heavy comforter completely over my head and arms and rolled me quick as a flash off the seat and down between the team and the load … Frank took one step but Bill stood as if rooted while I untangled myself from the quilt and finally managed to roll out and then pull out the quilt and finally get the lines straightened out." Not long after that experience, Luna had a baby girl.

"Jessie having gotten large enough so she was liable to kick out of the rocking chair we placed her in a cracker box with a little pillow in the bottom and a quilt around the top and sides to soften them … "

"Saturday night it rained J.T. fixed a canopy over the bed to keep the rain off from a quilt."

I was mighty proud of him and have never seen before or since such a handsome man. He had always worn white shirts as bridge foreman and I could not bear to see him in any others in the summer so always made them of unbleached muslin with linen cuffs and collars ——

SORROWS

In 1878, nine-month old James Alexander, "looked in my eyes and smiled and looked up over my head and smiled as if he saw something fine and I felt that he went from my arms to my mothers … We buried him in the yard we could not take our baby any too far."

In 1880, "The babies had been dying around us that summer with cholera infection … Susie (who was thirteen months old) began to sicken a little … so I put up some lunch and we made a holiday of it (going to the doctor). Susie sat on the seat between us when not on her fathers lap and whenever she saw pretty flowers on the prairie she would stretch out her hands for them and J.T. would stop and jump out and get them. We went home greatly relieved, but she did not get better. Before morning she died … My father drove to Juniata for the coffin … We laid Susie by our little boy."

After Susie died, Luna "had a constant and terrible headache and my hair was very long and extremely heavy so I thought it would relieve me to have it cut off. J.T. thought so too and as of course no one ever thought of going to a barber I would have to cut it and several times he got the shears but he would lift up my hair and say, 'I can't do it,' so one day when the pain seemed unbearable I took the shears and cut out a chunk and then took them out where he was plowing … he cut the rest of it but it did not do any good. Cutting hair will not cure a broken heart."

In the 1890s, the Kellie family purchased a printing press and began publishing the *Prairie Home,* a newsletter in support of the Farmers Alliance and the populist movement, with the stated aim "to secure for the laborer the full value of the wealth he creates." Widowed in 1919, Mrs. Kellie was visiting a daughter in Phoenix, Arizona, when she decided to take up a 640-acre homestead. She was in her 70s.

Sod house homemaker Luna Sanford Kellie died at the age of 82 and is buried beside her husband, J.T., in Heartwell, Nebraska.

Maria Jane Forsythe Newton

1836 – 1933

*"I have got Harold, Ralph quilt top done and gave to them.
Got Lye's done ready to join. Have all my grandchildren done. Thirty one. That is a lot of piecing
but something they will remember me everytime they see the quilt."* [19]

Grandmother Newton was
a 59-year-old widow when she left
Ohio to join family in Nebraska.

FAMILY PHOTOGRAPH
COURTESY OF DR. LEO LEMONDS

Born near McConnelsville, Ohio, in 1836, Maria Jane Forsythe was nineteen years old when she married Abel Newton on October 2, 1855. The couple would eventually have twelve children, all of them born on Newton Ridge near Stockport, Ohio.

Maria Jane gave birth to her fifth child only a month after Abel was drafted into Company I, 78th Regiment of the Ohio Voluntary Infantry. While Abel was away, the wife he called "Jince" and his children worked their one-and-a-half acre garden, cut wood, and cared for the family's two cows and chickens. The family was working in the field one day in 1865 when they spied an old man coming towards them. The children didn't recognize their father, but Maria Jane looked up and "went to meet him on the run." Abel's health would never fully recover from his Civil War service.

Maria Jane's parents and several of her grown children had already immigrated to Furnas County, Nebraska, when, in 1884, Abel died "of a lung ailment." The Newtons had already planned to join the rest of the family in Nebraska prior to his death, and so it was that, in the spring of 1885, as a fifty-nine-year-old widow, Mrs. Newton and the five children still living at home headed west. After a brief homesteading experience in Kansas, Mrs. Newton took up residence in the sod house originally built by her father. She subsequently added on a log house.

The Newtons were faithful correspondents, intent on maintaining family ties. Descendents treasure the thousand-plus letters that illuminate their ancestors' lives. Both letters and family memories of Grandmother Newton reveal a beloved, hard-working matriarch who's textile production included not only quilt-making but also shearing sheep, carding wool, spinning yarn, cloth, making clothing, and weaving carpet strips.

In 1896, Grandmother Newton's daughter, Ella Rush, wrote her sister Alice, "we are going to piece Ma a silk quilt for her birthday, crazy work … The blocks are 19x24 in. … I got enough [remnants] of a milliner in Beaver … to cover 15 in. square just laid down touching each other for 5 cents. I will send you the directions … I can send you a few pieces for your block if you want me to. Do not say any thing about this in Ma's letter."

Grandmother Newton was one of a group of "very good quilters" at Bethel Church in Stamford, Nebraska, who quilted once a week (when not too busy on the farm) to earn money for missions. The group often worked on two quilts at a time, with three ladies seated on each side of frames boasting six-foot long poles.

Maria Jane Forsythe Newton died at home on December 11, 1933. She was 97.

FAMILY PHOTOGRAPH COURTESY OF DR. LEO LEMONDS

Both Grandmother Newton's letters and those by other family members show that quilt-making was an important part of her life.

From Grandmother Newton's Letters

*"Albert bought a house pattern. Four rooms.
It would be placed near the orchard the other
side of the old sod house."*

"Election is over and I don't know whether the women get to vote here or not. If they do they will do away with liquor and saloons. That would be one good thing and they never will when the men vote for there is too many that drink."

*"I put in a quilt for Lola today Jennie
and I will quilt on it till we get it out."*

*"Wednesday I had the other quilt
in I have made for you.
So Grace, Lora and Elsie came over
and we took it out.
It is for a summer quilt.
Did not put any batten in it. An old blanket.
Did not put much quiltain on it.
If I don't come this summer will send it."*

From Grandmother Newton's Letters

"I am piecing a quilt for Claud."

"I went and voted for Hoover. I did not want Smith to get it for two reasons. He is for Whiskey and Catholic. We did not want either one of that in the White House … I went upstairs and swept all the rooms. Won't do any more to them till after Christmas. I don't do much sewing. Made Perley four pare mittens. I have a waist and apron to make for myself. The quilt I pieced for Girty. Elsie and me quilted it in when Lib was here."

"Azelia you had better stay with your mother till she gets well. Remember God only gives us one mother and what is home without a mother. Do all you can to help her. She is getting old and cant do as she used to."
(Grandmother Newton is 92 … Azelia is 71)

"You will both have to get in bed earlier than you have been. You are both getting old and need more rest … "

"Alice you ought to know you can't work all day and night. You are getting old and what will the boys do when you are gone. We don't iron towels or lots of things. So you boys don't let Alice iron your everyday shirts or underwear. Some days my side hurts then better but is better than it was. It will be a long time getting well. My ankles are most well. I am sending this sod house picture so you can show it to people that never saw one."

The Family about their aging Grandmother Newton:
"Grandma is feeling real well (has a time with her stomach occasionally). She looked so much better when come from Ohio than when she went. Sure a wonderful person for ninety one years old."

"We were at Grandma's for supper … I thought Grandma seemed very well. She has a quilt in as usual."

"Yes it is remarkable how well Grandma keeps going and doesn't have a girl. Says she doesn't want one."

"We were down to Grandma's this evening. She is getting weaker, her side still hurts her … She is still sitting up in chair or bed. Can not get her to lie down."

In 1885, Grandmother Newton moved into a Nebraska sod house originally built by her father.

Above: Wedding Ring signature quilt made by Grandmother Newton. The family remembers that she loved working with blue and white. According to Barbara Brackman's *Encyclopedia of Pieced Quilt Patterns*, the Wedding Ring block was first published by the Ladies Art Company in either 1889 or 1895.

PART TWO

Settling In

"I got busy making a small cupboard for the dishes and victuals … out of an Arbuckle coffee box, about the size of an ordinary trunk … I could use the saw and hammer very cleverly, it didn't take me long before I had two or three shelves in the cupboard and a nice white cloth nailed to the top of the box, dropping down for a door."[1]

NEBRASKA STATE HISTORICAL SOCIETY RG2608.PH1468

The Blair (or was it Huckleberry? The photographer's note indicates both names) family lived near Broken Bow, Nebraska, in 1888. Note that the girls are wearing dresses made from the same material.

NEBRASKA STATE HISTORICAL SOCIETY RG2608.PHI468

Following fairly common practice, Uriah Oblinger left his family behind when he headed west to establish a homestead. His wife, Mattie, and daughter, Ella, were to join him when he had a home built. In a February, 1873, letter to Mattie, he optimistically noted that " … with a $500 investment … ," a man could have "a good comfortable home in a beautiful looking country."[4] Uriah wasn't the first, nor would he be the last, to enthusiastically embrace the promise of his own homestead and a prosperous future. The Oblingers would have to do without essentials as well as luxuries and would have to employ creative solutions to achieve these dreams.

The Oblingers' hopeful outlook notwithstanding, many western women began housekeeping in a dugout. The Bartos family, who immigrated to Saline County from Czechoslovakia in 1885, is one example. The eight Bartos children and their mother did most of the digging to create their first home, a 20-foot by 24-foot one room dugout. "The ground served as a floor. The only entrance was a door facing the east and two windows, one next to the door and the other facing south." The family's beds, "made from crudely-formed native lumber," featured "straw-filled ticking. If straw wasn't available, corn husks were used." Eggs sold for a nickel a dozen, butter cost ten cents a pound, and calico cost three cents a yard.[5]

Mattie Oblinger's husband promised her a house.

"Well ma I will soon have the house done. I have the walls up the door frame in the pole up the middle the ridge pole on and the rafters up now I have the roof to put on yet, and a window to put in and the floor to level off and then it is ready to move into it is 14 by 16 foot inside the walls are 2½ ft thick I have worked a little over 9 days at it & hauled the sod and done every bit of work alone …[6]

Mattie brought at least one quilt with her to her Nebraska soddy. Uriah teased her about it:

"Well it must have been quite a surprise to you to get such a quilt it looks as though some one else thought something of you as well as me but you ought not to have told me about any of the mens names that were on it for I might get jealous you know but I will forgive them this time and thank them to boot, and all the Dear Ladies too & we'll try and think of all of them when we sleep under it.[7]

Close up detail: The treadle sewing machine revolutionized women's lives. In March of 1878, Mattie Oblinger wrote, "Mother can you do your sewing on the machine I wish I was near enough for a while to do some sewin on I have so much to do I do not know where to commence … we have the nicest sweetest prettiest and most mischievous girls in the state I know."[2] The following September, she wrote, "I think my work will not crowd me so much now. I had to make some new clothes for the girls to wear to the fair, and I was very much hurried as I done it all by hand. Mother, I often wish I was close to your machine for three girls makes lots of sewin."[3]

Mattie doesn't seem to have minded housekeeping in a 14-foot by 16-foot space with a dirt floor, although she was looking forward to her husband's building a larger place in the fall. She wrote home that her new sod house could be very comfortable, with "… nice walls and then plaster and lay a floor above and below." The dirt-floored soddy from which she wrote that letter would then become "a nice comfortable stable."[8]

Women's reactions to living in a sod house were as varied as the women who came west. Luna Kellie "had thought a sod house would be kind of nice, but the sight of the first one sickened me."[9] Grace McCance doesn't record her mother's reaction to the soddy Charles McCance built for his young family, but she doesn't seem to have minded the one she moved into over a dozen years later as Mrs. Bert Snyder—a four room soddy sitting in the middle of an unfenced yard of bunchgrass and prickly-pear cactus. "It had a corrugated tin roof, wood floors and ceiling, plastered walls, and double-sashed windows. I could hardly wait to get started fixing it up."[10]

Like Grace Snyder, most homemakers seemed to be interested in "fixing up" their surroundings. Solomon Butcher's photographic record reveals lace curtains at sod house windows, flowers blooming on the deep windowsills, and beautiful quilts adorning beds.

Katie Goar Maze, who arrived in Nebraska in 1883, recounts a fairly typical story of settling in:

"We divided our new house 20 x 14, into two rooms. Deep windows at each end of the rooms gave us plenty of sunlight and made a fine place for my flowers and potted plants. Our furniture was that which my mother had given us in Indiana, and the carpet the one I had woven on my mother's loom.

"I got busy making a small cupboard for the dishes and victuals. It was made out of an Arbuckle coffee box, about the size of an ordinary trunk ... Next morning, I was up early and baked pancakes for breakfast ... we ate our breakfast out-of-doors ..."[11]

Some improvements were about more than beauty. Mrs. Thompson Lamphere of York County recalled, "My mother lined the roof with wool blankets tacked up to prevent bits of hay or tiny clods of dirt falling down on us in windy weather."[12]

Obtaining potable water was often a challenge. The Goars traveled half a mile to the nearest well until they could dig their own, which Mrs. Maze says "was about 152 feet deep" and dug by hand. The Oblingers had a small pond nearby, but had to go a quarter of a mile for drinking water.

Once settled, homesteading women quickly set about planting their kitchen gardens. Mattie Oblinger planted squashes, cucumbers, melons, beans, potatoes (ten bushels of seed potatoes), tomatoes, beets, and cabbage ("I set a hundred and thirty cabbages last week"[13]). While Mattie gardened her husband was planting sod corn, "he will soon have 40 acres turned over."[14]

In addition to planting huge gardens, sod house homemakers took advantage of wild fruits and berries.

Katie Maze wrote ...

"We often went fruit picking. In short time, our baskets and buckets were filled with delicious berries; chokecherries and black raspberries being especially abundant. We purchased cherry seeders and canned many quarts. When cooked, the chokecherries lost their bitter flavor. Buffalo berries, which grew on small trees along the Loup River bank, made fine jelly, as did the wild gooseberries, currants, and plums."[15]

Establishing a flock of chickens, especially laying hens, and planting fruit trees was often a priority.

In July of 1885, new settler Julia Baptist wrote ... "I did not answer your letter before now because I have not had time I have been busy tending to my chickens and one thing and another . . . it was a little windy some days when we first got here but now I don't see any difference from back there . . . this is a good country for any thing that [a] person puts in the ground to come up . . .we put out thirty six apple trees this spring and some small fruit black berries straw berries our well is two hundred and nineteen feet deep it cost seventy six dollars besides the wind mill to east one hundred fifty dollars."[16]

Finding fuel on a mostly treeless prairie presented a challenge. "What could we burn?" wrote Mrs. Lizzie Wirt. "Cornstalks cut like cord wood back home. After a windy day we gathered tumble weeds that lodged near our house. Then buffalo 'chips' were good—they lasted longer than the tumbleweed and cornstalks ..."[17]

Many women had close encounters of the unwanted kind with a variety of varmints. Mrs. H. J. Yeck of Custer County related her nighttime experience with a bull snake. After having aired the bedding one afternoon on the grass she told of feeling something cold and clammy in the night. When she mentioned it to her husband ... He said, "It's just your imagination, go to sleep. I worried for a while and then got up, but not finding anything went back to bed ... In the morning I got up to dress and I heard something go k-plop on the floor. Looking around there was a big bull snake three and a half feet long. He had fallen out of my bed, and was scrambling and trying to get away . . . Mr. Snake was quickly dispatched and carried out of door."[18]

Deprivation was common. At least some of the time, Mattie Oblinger seems to have had the ability to gain some perspective on her situation, as evidenced in this letter to

Quilts endured and, whether treasured by descendents or donated to museums, all remain as silent witnesses to the process of arriving ... settling in ... and staying on.

her sister (reproduced here with Mattie's creative spelling and punctuation intact) …

"Yesterday morning I thought I would have some cakes for dinner. I was going to make Jumbles but Giles had not rolling pin or cake cutter so I made a plate of pancakes as we always term it well I had no eggs but I thought I would try it with out I'll tell you what I used nearly a teacup of sugar about half teacup of cream filled up with water makeing teacup ful of cream & water a small lump of butter and a little soda enough flour to make quite stuff and I never made any better pancake in my life try it some time I make Pancakes altogether without eggs We used to think if we had no eggs we could not make Pancakes but I have got bravely over that try it some time take equal parts of sour & sweet milke soda nad salt and see how nice and light they are it is my way of makeing them."[19]

Children were expected to help out, and many put in long hours helping plant gardens and tend livestock. One remembered …

"At first, we had no fences and, as the cattle must have pasture, it fell to my lot to watch them graze. Dinner time was the only time that I came home. You may be very sure it became very monotonous, and I tried to pass the time away by reading, piecing quilt blocks, and hunting wild flowers. At evening we would catch the cows and hobble them down by the house."[20]

Hard as "settling in" to a sod house might have been, not everything was bleak.

While diaries and letters home reveal homesickness and deprivation, they also mention socializing, games, literary societies, dances, and church meetings. Maggie Oblinger Sandon remembered, "Winter evenings we would play Authors or Dominoes or Checkers." The family made their own dominoes from an empty soda box. She commented, "Authors were our delight and it taught us so many of the old-time authors and what books they had written … "[21]

Grace McCance and her sisters made entire families of corn husk dolls.

Maggie Sandon received a cherished doll in 1888 and said, "I was enthralled with the dolls. Aunt May was to buy one for me but I did not know that. When in the store I kept hanging around the doll counter … I had fallen in love with a blue-eyed one with blond curls. Head, hands and feet were made of what was called bisque. Painted so the face looked natural. Sleepy eyes. Aunt May got it for me without me seeing the transaction … All presents were taken to the church those days and put on the Xmas tree. I was all eyes but could not see it any place. I almost stopped breathing but at last it was taken off from some place and my name called. I don't know if I walked or floated when I went up to claim it … What delightful times I had sewing for that doll. The blue satin was laid away so carefully and put on only on very special occasions. She was never thrown down carelessly."[22]

Mrs. Cora Ellis Austin of York County, Nebraska, remembered the dances …

"In the winter time, no matter how cold the weather, we would bundle up and climb into the straw-filled lumber wagon, with plenty of quilts and blankets and drive to Uncle Will's … He lived in a sod house and his two sisters, Laura and Lydia kept house for him. Lydia played the violin and could dance and jig with the best of them. Will and Steve and Lydia played for dances and I used to 'chord' for them on the organ some times."[23]

Quilts in wagons, quilts in trunks, quilts as parting gifts, quilts as entertainment while herding cattle … Quilts endured and, whether treasured by descendents or donated to museums, all remain as silent witnesses to the process of arriving … settling in … and staying on.

Grace McCance Snyder

1882-1982

"When the sun had warmed the air enough that I could take my mittens off,
I sat in my straw nests and sewed on the little quilt,
making my stitches small and neat so Mama would let me have more pieces."[24]

No discussion of sod house homemakers would be complete without mention of Quilters Hall of Fame member Grace McCance Snyder, whose Petit-Point Flower Basket and Mosaic quilts were included in *The 20th Century's 100 Best American Quilts*. Grace McCance was three years old when, in 1885, she and her mother and two sisters stepped off the train in Cozad, Nebraska, to join their husband and father who'd come to Nebraska three months earlier, filed on a quarter-section, and built a 12-foot by 14-foot sod house. Grace's mother made curtains from bleached flour sacks on which she'd embroidered flying red birds, created shelves from cigar boxes, and, for a time, managed to feed her family without milk, eggs, or butter.

Appointed as herder to her father's cattle, Grace begged fabric scraps from her mother and made her first quilt, a four-patch doll quilt, while on duty. Quilt making would be a welcome distraction through many long winters throughout Grace's life. When hired to teach the two sons of a ranch family living in a three room soddy, Grace saw no one but her employer and her two students for days on end. Her employer would not allow Grace to help with any of the housework. From the time she left the schoolroom until bedtime, she had nothing to do. Looking back on that long winter, she said that the fact that she'd purchased fabric

She exhibited her quilts at national and international quilt shows, winning blue and purple ribbons.

before heading to the ranch and could work on a quilt likely saved her sanity.

By the time she was twenty-one, Grace was convinced that she would never be a bride and decided to go back to school and work on her second-grade certificate. When she'd finished, her father encouraged her to come home and look for work. Grace hesitated. When a friend invited her to a fish fry, she met a cowboy named Bert Snyder. It wasn't long before the new Mrs. Bert Snyder was setting up housekeeping in her cowboy's four room soddy. She spent her first morning there lining her cupboard shelves with newspaper she'd trimmed with scalloped edges. Two broomsticks pounded into the sod wall with a board across them created a living room table. A wire cot became a couch, once padded with old blankets and covered with one of Grace's quilts. The quilt she'd made during the long winter teaching two boys on a ranch graced a spare bed she made from an old bedspring and canned goods boxes.

The first spring after her wedding, when the baby she was expecting was stillborn, Grace blamed herself for taking a long, hard buggy trip and spending hours at her sister-in-law's treadle sewing machine to create a new dress trimmed with dozens of rows of fine tucks. Her baby was laid to rest wrapped in "a lovely little featherstitched silk doll quilt that Aunt Ollie had given me years before."

The Snyders had been

married four years before Grace got her own sewing machine, earning the money by raising an orphaned calf. The couple ordered their winter supplies from the Montgomery Wards catalogue that August. In September, Bert would head for town after the order. Because hauling everything sometimes required three or four round-trips, Grace reminded her husband to bring her sewing machine on the first load, "no matter what." While Bert was gone, she cut and basted a pile of clothes for her two children. Imagine Grace's excitement when Bert arrived after dark and she helped him unload the crate by moonlight. Imagine her disappointment when she realized that the crate contained only the cabinet. The head, shipped in a separate crate, was still waiting at the train depot.

When the time came for the two oldest Snyder daughters to attend high school, Bert and Grace rented out the ranch and traveled to Salem, Oregon, where Bert's sister, Alice, lived. Grace joined Alice's neighborhood quilting club. Her letters to married daughter, Nellie, mention Grace's finishing a red, green, and white Saw Tooth quilt, starting a Double Wedding Ring, working on a Log Cabin, and beginning a Necktie quilt.

When her girls graduated from high school in Oregon and did not return to the ranch, Grace set her quilting frames up in their room. These were the years she would

Grace and Bert Snyder, their wedding photograph dated October 23, 1903.

PHOTO COURTESY OF BISON BOOKS

create her "show quilts." She finished the Mosaic Hexagon and the Basket Petit Point, exhibiting her quilts at national and international quilt shows, winning blue and purple ribbons, and filling a scrapbook with magazine and newspaper articles about her quilts.

When 18 of Grace's quilts were hung in the Fine Arts building at the Nebraska State Fair, she overheard someone musing aloud that the quilt maker must not have had anything else to do but make quilts. Speaking of that incident, Grace said, "At the time I made all the quilts in that display, I was still living on the ranch, baking our bread, churning our butter, making my own soap, and raising a big garden every summer … "

While the soddies she inhabited have long ago disappeared, Grace McCance Snyder's legacy lives on, both in the stunning quilts she created and in the land where she and hundreds like her put down roots and grew a life.

Rachel Rice Newton

Iowa resident Rachel Rice Newton married Charles Newton of Antelope County, Nebraska, in 1879. The Newtons homesteaded in a sod house 11 miles south of Oakdale, Nebraska. Charles filed homestead exemption #4676 November 13, 1884. Below and opposite: Mrs. Newton hand-pieced the fan quilt blocks. Shirley Burkhead, the wife of Mrs. Newton's great-grandson, received the quilt top in the 1970s and finished quilting it in 2004-2005.

FAMILY PHOTOGRAPH ABOVE COURTESY OF MR. AND MRS. EUGENE BURKHEAD

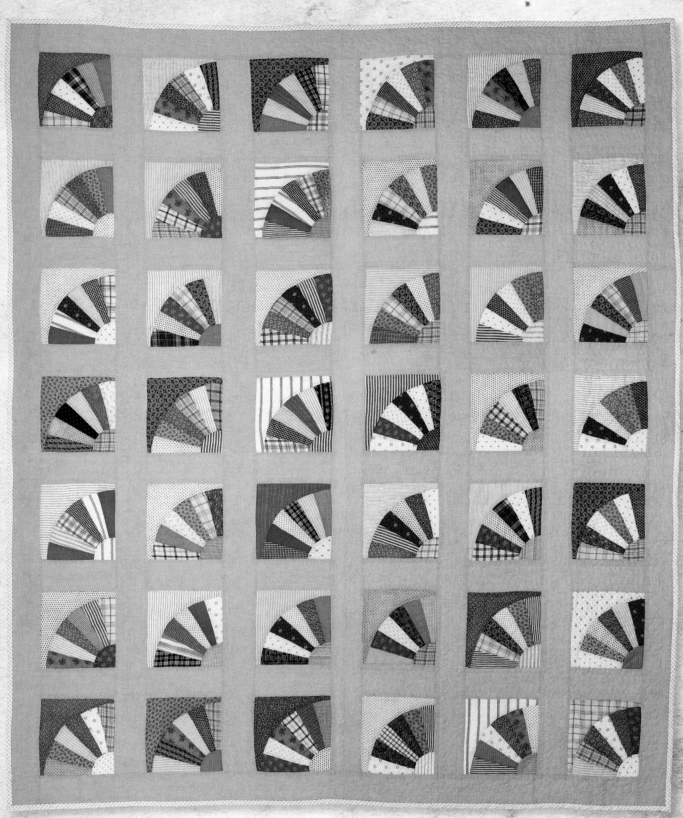

Mrs. Newton's five children were born between 1880 and 1895, several while she lived in the soddy. The fabrics used in the top suggest it may have been made during her "sod house homemaking" days. According to Barbara Brackman's *Encyclopedia of Pieced Quilt Patterns,* the Fan Patchwork block (which Brackman assigns entry #3307 in her book) was first published by the Ladies Art Company in 1897 as their pattern #296.

PART THREE

Staying On

"Na, we're ance here and we're nae to gae back."[1]

Above: These Custer County, Nebraska, girls look like they dressed up to have their picture taken. Right, close up detail: Notice the scrap quilt on the bed as you peek through the doorway.

Mention the word "pioneer," and most Americans picture heroic men and women forging a new life and staying on their newly acquired homesteads "come heck or high water." The truth is much more complicated. Sod house pioneers who stayed on had to survive financial panics and drought, hordes of Rocky Mountain locusts, blizzards and the loss of children in numbers thankfully unfamiliar to twenty-first century mothers. As the 19th century wore on, many homesteaders packed up and left.

Those who stayed on and their offspring cherished those eventful years as sod house pioneers. They understood the significance of their accomplishments. Nebraska photographer Solomon Butcher preserved their experiences in photographs. Photographic essays and websites abound cataloging these documents.

The children and grandchildren of Nebraska pioneers collected memoirs, testimonials, letters, diaries and personal papers documenting a wide variety of pioneer experiences. It is from these materials, housed at the Nebraska State Historical Society, that we learned so much about the women who came west with hope and forbearance in their hearts to make a new life. We close our tribute with their words.

"Our house was a sod one of two rooms and a cave. The first room had a wooden floor on it. The second room was nothing but a dirt floor … The first room was a level ground room, the second room went back into the side of the hill. In 1876 … we had a grasshopper plague … they almost darkened the sun. Then they began descending and in a few minutes they were at work in the cornfields. You could hear them plainly as they gnawed … Mrs. Myers tried to save the garden by placing carpets and quilts over the plants but it was useless as they ate every bit of the garden".[2]

"Little Cecil was the first child to be buried in our new cemetery … the morning after my little nephew died, I had a premonition that my baby would be next … in one week our darling was taken from us … Little had I thought, when Father felled a large poplar tree in his woods and made it into a large box which would just fit into the immigration car for my household effects that I was moving to Nebraska, that it would later be used for the rough box and casket for this child. … Black cotton cloth covered the casket outside and cheap white muslin was used to line the inside. We tacked narrow white lace around the edge inside. We had four such caskets trimmed in our home that fall."[3]

"One of the happiest times of my life was when I invited six ministers to my home for dinner. There were two rooms in my sod house, and I had a little Number Seven cook stove in a corner of the kitchen to cook on. My drop-leaf table, large enough for the six ministers, was placed in the middle of the kitchen. I was as busy as Martha with the preparation of the meal."

This young Nebraska girl may have had a difficult life by modern standards, but she didn't lack amusements.

Above: O.S. Welch Residence 4½ miles south of Berwyn, East Custer County, Nebraska, 1889 or 1890. Right, close up detail: Note the bed inside the door piled high with comforters.

"After the doctor had made the diagnosis, he decided to operate. He had me put the extra leaves in the kitchen table, spread a sheet over it, and get him some hot water and a clean dishpan. Having studied a little physiology, I asked Doc if he thought that was a sanitary place to operate. Doc grinned and said, 'Son, this woman is used to these germs— they won't hurt her,' and they didn't. He not only located and deleted the offending gall bladder, but took out her appendix for good measure, with the comment that he didn't want to have to drive back up here for that. The patient recovered and outlived the doctor."[5]

"If a girl hadn't started to piece a quilt by the time she was eight or ten years old we just didn't have anything to do with her."[6]

NEBRASKA STATE HISTORICAL SOCIETY RG2608.PH18030

Above: The photographer noted that this is the York family of West Union, Nebraska. He dated the photo 188?, and then added a fascinating and unsettling note: "Mr. York … in a debate on women's suffrage one time he said he did not believe in ladies voting. He thought the dear ladies should not have to bother their brain about pollitics. But sit in their parlor in an easy chair and direct their housework. It is said he would bring his wife home from the neighbors at the end of a black snake whip and whip her home when she stayed longer than he thought proper."

Left, close up detail: When you look in the window, you can see what appears to be a basket quilt on the bed.

"The visit of the peddler always was an occasion for excitement. In his especially equipped wagon he carried almost everything, and from his stock 'Mom' would choose the calico for her new dress and the goods for our Sunday pants and shirts. They usually carried combs, ornaments, buttons, thread, underwear, pots, pans, kitchenware, condiments, seasonings, and gimcracks for the kids."[7]

"George and I precipitated an acquaintance with Dr. and Mrs. Purdum, former residents of Abingdon, Ill. They lived in a dugout with a sod roof on which grew tall sunflowers and through which they thrust their stovepipe and in driving one Sunday afternoon we drove upon the roof and our pony stepped through before we knew we were on their dugout. A profound apology cemented our friendship."[9]

"I have commenced peicing a quilt I know no name for it it is peiced of dark & light calico I did think I would peice an Ocean wave but when I peice that I want it for a nice quilt I have seen some scrap quilts peiced that way here and they look real well."[8]

"Mother loved to work outside in the field rather than do housework … we girls were trained early in our lives to care for the house in order that Mother could drive a team in the field and help Dad on the farm. … It seemed, that when machinery broke down, Mother could figure out where and what the trouble was, much better than Dad could."[10]

"There were only ten women and forty men and we danced all night, and the men nearly danced us women to death — at a Calico Ball, the lady made a calico dress and a necktie to match it. The men were given a bunch of neckties and asked to choose one without seeing the lady whose dress it matched. In this way, original partners were selected."[11]

"Poor in material things, my mother was rich in loving neighborliness. For miles around the sick, dying and bereaved called for Julie Stevens to come. Leaving us children with neighbors, she'd be off with her team of ponies on an errand of mercy." [12]

"I have seen an entire field of corn green in the morning but so whipped by the hot dry winds that it lay in ruin by night." [13]

Top: According to the Custer County Historical Society, the correct spelling of the name noted by the photographer as "S.R. Conner" of Ansley, Nebraska," is actually Comer. In twenty-two years, Mary Comer (that is probably her seated in the wagon), gave birth to ten children. Above, close up detail: Note the quilts displayed on the fence.

Note the Crazy Quilt, Star Quilt, and Log Cabin (hanging above the canned goods) on display at the 1886 Custer County Fair held in Broken Bow, Nebraska. On September 30, 1879, sod house homemaker Mattie Oblinger wrote about attending two other county fairs in Nebraska: " … we have attended the Clay Co. and Fillmore Co. fairs … the Fillmore fair was splendid, was almost as good as the state fair from what we can learn … the display of quilts and other needlework was grand … "

And from a sod house homemaker's diary ...

"October 4, 1887 ... dance in John's new house. October 19, 1887 Quilted a Quilt. December 31, 1887 ... The last day of the old year. The day is cold and dreer. The storm is howling. No one is in today. All shivering around a cob fire. Yet we should not complain, for many would be glad of as good. Winter with his frosty breath is giving us a little of the Artic regions where he is supposed to hold his coast. May the coming year be a happy one and may we all be spared to the close." [14]

Grace Susannah Budd Wood

"...after she had worked all day in the field,
she would work until midnight making and mending clothing
for the children and doing the total needle-work for the family ..."[15]

Above: The photographer's caption spoke of "James Wood, an old timer and his wife, in front of their old sod house, Dale Valley, Nebraska, 1904." Subsequent research reveals that "the wife" had a name, too: Grace Susannah Budd Wood.

The corner of the soddy is just visible beyond the porch on the windmill side of the new house (built in 1904). Mrs. Wood is standing, hand on hip, on the far right.

Family history indicates this English paper-pieced quilt was likely made while Mrs. Wood lived in her sod house. Fabrics include late 19th century silk plaids and prints, and wool. The backing is a beautiful wool madder stripe.

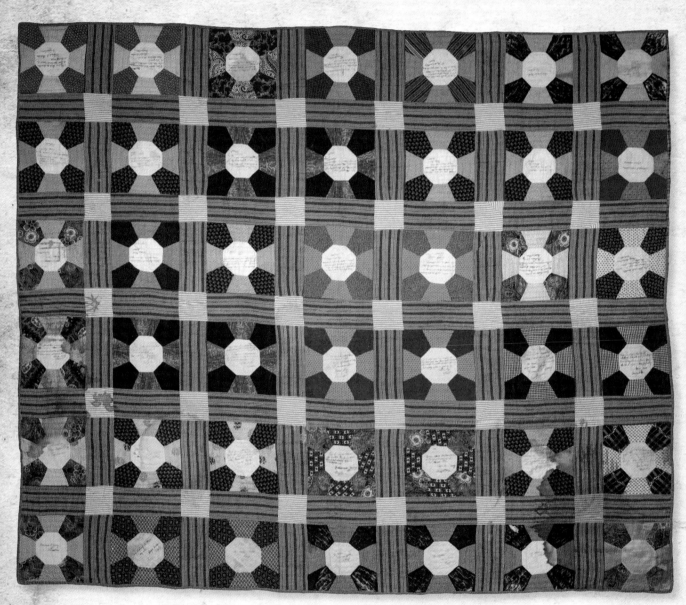

The first publication of the Wedge and Circle pattern can be dated to as early as 1885 in *Hearth and Home* magazine published in Augusta, Maine. Since the family knows this quilt was made for the couple's marriage in Nova Scotia in 1875, one wonders if this is one of the quilts that inspired the published pattern.

PHOTO BY AARON LEIMKUHLER, KANSAS CITY STAR

The writing reads:
"A union quilt you have begun
Ask a piece from everyone
If at the quilting I am not there
Think of the one that gave the square"

Manerva McWilliams Hersh and Margaret Alice Osborne Raney

Top: The Hersh family outside their sod house just east of Broken Bow, Nebraska. Minnie, inheritor of Granny Raney's beautiful quilt, is in the back row, third from the left. Minnie's daughter, Margaret, received the quilt as a wedding gift. It passed to Margaret's daughter in 1951, who subsequently donated it to the Nebraska State Historical Society.

Above, left: Margaret Alice Osborne (Granny) Raney promised her coveted quilt to her grandson's wife, Minnie, if the child Minnie was carrying was a girl and if Minnie named that baby girl Margaret. Above, right: Nebraska sod house homemaker Manerva "Minnie" McWilliams Hersh inherited Granny Raney's quilt as promised when she named the baby girl, who was born in 1878, Margaret. Granny Raney had passed away a few months prior to the baby's birth.

FAMILY PHOTOGRAPHS, COURTESY OF MR. AND MRS. DAN HERSH

When this quilt was donated to the Nebraska State Historical Society, the donor provided family history that indicates Margaret Alice Osborne made it during the first year after her 1827 marriage to George Raney. The quilt was then packed into the wagon the family used to migrate from Indiana to Missouri in 1841. Exactly when the quilt came to Nebraska is unknown.

Quilt Projects

Ward Family 9-Patch Doll Quilt

This lovely little doll quilt is an exact replication of quilt #2008.034.0300 from the Mary Ghormley collection at the International Quilt Study Center in Lincoln, Nebraska (searchable database: www.quiltstudy.org). The original quilt was made by Helen Polzin Ward, born in 1863 to German immigrant parents then living in Wisconsin. In 1870, the family moved to Nebraska, and family history suggests that Helen made the quilt sometime in the 1870s.

When Helen was 21 years old, she and a sister homesteaded on adjoining claims in the far northwest corner near the South Dakota border between Rushville and Gordon, Nebraska. They built a sod house straddling their claims so they could live together. According to family history, they lived so close to the Pine Ridge Indian Reservation that they could hear the gunfire from the battle of Wounded Knee in December 1890. That same year Helen met and married Martin Ward. They eventually moved to Rushville, NE.

The original quilt was made of double pink and indigo fabrics. An alternative red, white and blue quilt illustrates another color scheme.

INSTRUCTIONS
✳ For 20 pink print setting blocks, cut
✳ 2 – 3½" x 44" pink print strips. Cut into 20 – 3½" squares.

✳ For 20 blue and pink 9-patch blocks, cut
✳ 5 – 1½" x 44" blue print strips
✳ 4 – 1½" x 44" pink print strips

FABRIC REQUIREMENTS
½ yard pink for setting blocks and 9-patch squares
½ yard indigo/blue for 9-patch squares, border and binding
¾ yard of fabric for backing
Batting – approximately 30" x 20"

Quilt Size: 17" x 26" • Block Size: 3" Finished
Doll Quilt made by Kathy Moore and quilted by Kathy Moore

✳ Sew
✳ 2 strip sets of blue-pink-blue strips (b-p-b)
✳ 1 strip set of pink-blue-pink (p-b-p) strips
✳ Cut across the strip sets in 1½" increments.

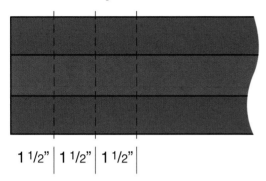

1 ½" | 1 ½" | 1 ½"

✳ Cut 40

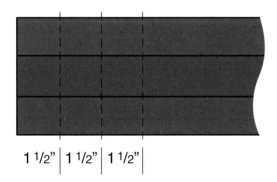

1 ½" | 1 ½" | 1 ½"

✳ Cut 20

✳ Sort into sets of 2 b-p-b and 1 p-b-p strip sets
✳ Make 20 – 9-patch blocks.

✳ Sew the 9-patch blocks and the setting blocks together into horizontal strips. Make 5 strips. Refer to the Setting Diagram for placement.

✳ Sew the rows together.

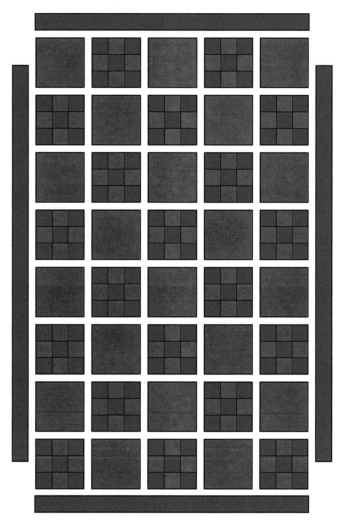

BORDERS

✳ Cut 2 – 1½" x 15½" strips (or measurement of quilt from side to side). Sew the strips to the top and bottom edges.

✳ Cut 2 – 1½" x 26½" strips (or measurement of quilt from top to bottom). Sew a strip to each side.

✳ Square up the top, if needed. Layer top, batting, backing, baste, quilt, and bind.

Quilt Size: 17" x 26" • Block Size: 3" Finished
Doll Quilt made by Kathy Moore and quilted by Linda Gosey

Heimer Family Snowball Quilt

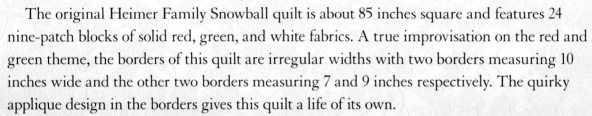

This unique red and green creation, circa 1870s, is one of several quilts donated to the Nebraska History Museum in the 1950s by Miss Octavia Heimer. The maker is unknown, but the family claimed Pennsylvania Dutch heritage. It is thought that Wesley Heimer brought this quilt with him when he came to Gordon, Nebraska, from Illinois in 1884. The unknown quilt maker left her mark on posterity with this and several other lively and original quilts now in the collection of the Nebraska History Museum in Lincoln.

The original Heimer Family Snowball quilt is about 85 inches square and features 24 nine-patch blocks of solid red, green, and white fabrics. A true improvisation on the red and green theme, the borders of this quilt are irregular widths with two borders measuring 10 inches wide and the other two borders measuring 7 and 9 inches respectively. The quirky applique design in the borders gives this quilt a life of its own.

We chose to bring this traditional pattern into the twenty-first century with a graphic combination of red, black and white. Vintage buttons echo the original maker's stylized border while providing a way to showcase treasured reminders of the past.

INSTRUCTIONS

❊ From the black print, cut
❊ 20 – 3½" squares

❊ From white, cut
❊ 16 – 3½" squares
❊ 80 – 1⅛" squares

❊ From red, cut
❊ 64 – 1⅛" squares

❊ The wall hanging is comprised of four 9-inch finished blocks based on the common 9-patch. The contrasting corners provide a secondary design.

❊ Each of the four 9-inch finished blocks is made up of 4 light "snowballs" with red corners and 5 dark "snowballs" with white corners. You will need to make a total of 20 black snowballs and 16 white to make the quilt.

FABRIC REQUIREMENTS

1 yard black print for blocks, border vine, and binding
⅜ yard red
1 yard white
1 yard for backing
29" square batting
8 buttons – 4 round and 4 triangular

❋ For each snowball:

❋ Draw a stitching line diagonally across four of the 1⅛" squares.

Dotted line is stitching line

❋ With right sides together, align a 1⅛" square in each corner of the 3½" square.

❋ Stitch each of the four small squares in place following the diagonal stitching line.

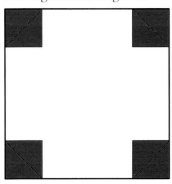

❋ Trim corner away leaving ¼" seam allowance.

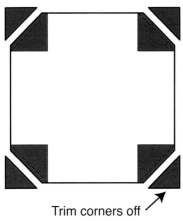

Trim corners off

❋ Press the seam allowance toward the center. You now have a completed snowball.

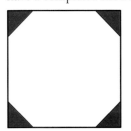

❋ Follow this procedure and make 20 black snowballs with white triangles and 16 white snowballs with red triangles.

BLOCK ASSEMBLY

❋ For each of the four blocks:

❋ Create three rows of snowballs alternating the dark and light blocks.

❋ Sew the 3 rows together to make one snowball nine-patch block.

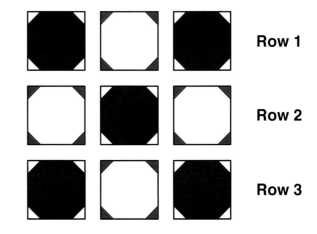

Row 1

Row 2

Row 3

❋ Make four snowball 9-patch blocks.

❋ Trim each block to measure 9½".

Quilt Size: 29" square • Block Size: 9" Finished
Quilt made and quilted by Stephanie Whitson

Heimer Family Snowball Quilt continued

BORDERS AND SASHING

* From the red fabric, cut
* 2 – 1½ x 9½" strips for center sashing
* 3 – 1½" x 19½" strips for top and bottom borders
* 2 – 1½" x 22½" strips inner side borders

* From white fabric, cut
* 2 – 4½" x 22½" strips for top and bottom borders
* 2 – 4½" x 29½" strips for side borders

* Follow the diagram on page 55 and sew the blocks, sashing and borders together.

* From the black print fabric, cut and sew enough 1" bias strips together to make 130" of bias for the vine.

* Press under ¼" along each raw edge of bias strip for the border vine.

* Refer to the photo on page 53 and appliqué the vine in place in a whimsical fashion.

* Layer the top, batting and backing together then quilt and bind.

* Sew the buttons in place.

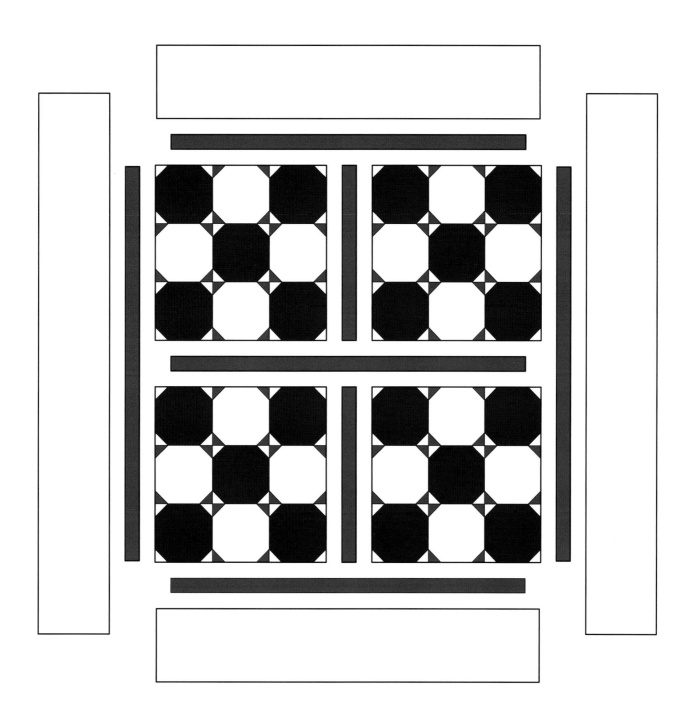

Grandmother Newton's "Laws O Massey" Quilt

Very few letters and diaries written by nineteenth century women mention quilts they've made. It is extremely rare to find quilts mentioned by pattern name until very late in the century when quilt patterns began to be published commercially. Improvisation was rampant in quilt making during most of the nineteenth century. Consequently, there are often many variations on a particular design theme that can be found in mid-to-late twentieth century quilt pattern indexes.

Such is the case with the original indigo and white quilt that Maria Jane Forsythe Newton called "Laws O Massey." She came to Nebraska in 1885 as a fifty-nine-year-old widow with five of her children. They lived in a sod house originally built by her father in Furnas County. At some point, she added a log-built addition. She particularly liked to make blue and white quilts, one of which is featured here.

This quilt, which is a unique variation on a nine-patch, has a very unique name. Grandmother Newton always called it the "Laws O Massey" quilt. The phrase may be a derivation of "lord 'a mercy" or "lands 'a mercy" both of which probably devolved from the phrase, "Lord have mercy." A search of the internet and quilt pattern indexes has not, as yet, found Grandmother Newton's pattern by any name.

INSTRUCTIONS
Each block is made using one Unit A and four Unit B. The directions are for each block. Make 9.

❋ Unit A
❋ From a blue fat quarter, cut
❋ 5 – 4" squares
❋ 1 – 1¾" x 18" strip

❋ From white fabric, cut
❋ 2 – 1 ⅝" x 18" strips

FABRIC REQUIREMENTS
9 fat quarters of assorted blues
4 yards white for blocks, sashing, borders and binding
3¾ yard for backing
67" square for batting

Quilt Size: 61" • Block Size: 15" Finished
Quilt made by Kathy Moore and quilted by Rich O'Hare.

❋ Make one white-blue-white strip set and cut into 4 – 4" increments.

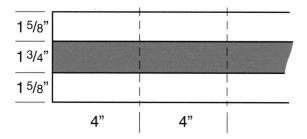

❋ Sew the strip sets and the squares together as shown in the diagram below.

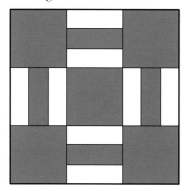

❋ Unit B: Make 4 per block.
❋ From the same blue fat quarter as used in Unit A, cut
❋ 24 – 2" squares

❋ From the white fabric, cut
❋ 12 – 2" squares

❋ To make the side and corner setting triangles:
❋ From the white fabric, cut
❋ 6 – 3½" squares.
❋ Cut each square from corner to corner twice on the diagonal to make 24 side setting triangles.

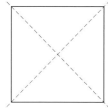

❋ From the white fabric, cut
❋ 2 – 2¼" squares

❋ Cut each square from corner to corner once on the diagonal to make 4 corner triangles.

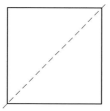

❋ Sew the squares and side setting triangles into rows as follows (refer to the diagram below):

❋ Row 1: 5 alternating blue and white squares. Begin and end the row with a white side setting triangle.

❋ Row 2: 3 alternating blue and white squares. Begin and end the row with a white side setting triangle.

❋ Row 3: 1 blue square. Begin and end the row with a white side setting triangle.

❋ Sew a white corner triangle to the unit. Refer to the diagram below.

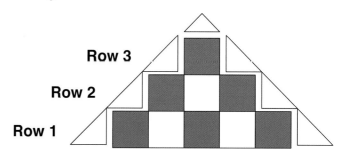

Row 3

Row 2

Row 1

❋ Sew a B unit to each side of an A unit as shown below.

❋ Trim the block if necessary to measure 15½" square.

BORDERS AND SASHING

✳ From the white fabric, cut

✳ 6 – 4½" x 15½" vertical sashing strips

✳ 3 – 4½" strips. Make two horizontal sashing strips 53½" long (or the measurement of the quilt top from side to side).

✳ Make 3 horizontal rows of three blocks incorporating the vertical sashing strips where shown in the assembly diagram below.

✳ Sew the rows to the horizontal sashing strips to complete the center of the quilt.

✳ From the white fabric, cut

✳ 3 – 4½" strips. Make two border strips that are 53½" long (or measurement of quilt from side to side). Sew the strips to the top and bottom of the quilt.

✳ 4 – 4½" strips. Make two border strips that are 61½" long (or the measurement of the quilt from top to bottom). Sew the strips to the sides.

✳ Square up the top, if needed. Layer top, batting, backing, baste, quilt, and bind.

Sageser Family Pomegranate Quilt

Often used in nineteenth century red and green quilts, the pomegranate design was also known as the "love apple." It may have evolved from the decorative pineapple motif thought to represent hospitality and was favored for use as a wedding quilt motif. One has to wonder if its use in wedding quilts led to the "love apple" designation or vice versa.

Our version of the Pomegranate comes from the family of Catherine Eby Miller. Family history in the documentation files of the Nebraska History Museum suggests it was made about 1855 by Catherine and that it came west with her daughter, Elizabeth Miller Sageser, to Chambers, Nebraska, in 1886 where it was used in a sod house by Elizabeth and her husband, Albert. Interestingly, because of confusing family history which contrasts with the evidence inherent in the quilts contained in this small collection, it is entirely possible that Catherine's mother, Susanette Eby, was actually the maker of this and other quilts in this collection.

Her pattern displays the innovative artistic approach of someone untrained in the fine arts; a characteristic common to mid- and late-nineteenth century American quilters. The beauty of these quilts comes as much from their natural and lively presentation as from the chosen colors. One can well imagine the joy and beauty they brought to the dark and dreary sod houses they decorated.

Catherine's original quilt measures 75½" square and is composed of nine blocks and sashing. Each block is 16½" square. Catherine chose to contain her blocks with sashing strips of a green print measuring one and three-quarters inches. There are red cornerstones at the intersections of the sashing. She framed her composition with a two-inch interior border, also a green print, and finished with an 8¾" outer border of the white background fabric. The narrow binding is of a green print calico. The quilting designs are random and consist of free form organic shapes – pomegranates, flowers, leaves and feathers.

INSTRUCTIONS

Our patterns assume basic piecing, appliqué, and quilting skills. Beginning quilters may refer to the many Kansas City Star books which provide excellent how-to instructions. Additionally, classes offered through local quilt guilds and shops are also an excellent way to learn the basics.

The measurements and templates included in this edition are drawn directly from Catherine's quilt. They can be reduced or enlarged according to your preferences, but for simplicity's sake, we recommend those just learning to appliqué begin with the larger version.

We hope you will be inspired by her quilts to try a relaxing and very portable sewing technique. As you are doing so, think of Catherine and her pioneering "prairie sisters."

We departed from Catherine's nine-block plan by arranging four blocks radiating out from the center. We also chose a green outer border for a little more contrast.

FABRIC REQUIREMENTS

1¼ yards light muslin

¾ yard dark green print for appliqué

⅓ yard green print for stems

¼ yard yellow print for appliqué

¼ yard red print for appliqué

¼ yard green print for inner border

3½ yards of fabric for backing

Batting – approximately 60" square

INSTRUCTIONS

✳ From the light muslin fabric, cut

✳ 4 – 18" squares

✳ When cutting the appliqué pieces, refer to the templates on pages 66-67.

✳ You will also need to cut the following:

✳ 4 – ⅞" x 16" green stems cut on the bias

✳ 8 – ⅞" x 8½" green stems cut on the bias

✳ Refer to the placement guide below and appliqué the pieces in place.

✳ Trim and square up the blocks to 17½".

SASHING AND BORDERS

✳ After the appliquéd blocks have been trimmed, cut

✳ 4 – 2½" x 17½" green sashing strips.

✳ 1 – 2½" red square.

✳ Sew a sashing strip to either side of the red square.

✳ Sew an appliquéd block to either side of a green sashing strip.

✳ Sew the three rows together to make the center of the quilt. Refer to the placement diagram below if necessary.

✳ From the red fabric, cut

✳ 2 – 1½" x 36½" strips (or measurement of quilt from side to side). Sew the strips to the top and bottom of the quilt.

✳ 2 – 1½" x 38½" strips (or measurement of quilt from top to bottom). Sew the strips to either side of the quilt.

✳ From the green fabric, cut

✳ 2 – 5½" x 38½" strips (or measurement of quilt from side to side). Sew the strips to the top and bottom of the quilt.

✳ 3 – 5½" strips. Make two border strips that are 48½" long(or measurement of quilt from top to bottom). Sew the strips to either side of the quilt.

✳ Square up the top, if needed. Layer top, batting, backing, baste, quilt, and bind.

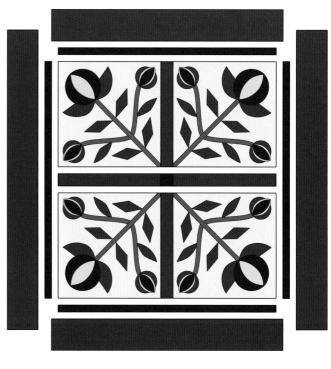

Quilt Size: 48" Square • Block Size: 17" Finished
Quilt made by Stephanie Whitson and quilted by Piecemakers of Lincoln, Nebraska

ON POINT ALTERNATIVE
FABRIC REQUIREMENTS

3½ yards light muslin for blocks,
   border and binding

¾ yard dark green print for appliqué

⅓ yard green print for stems

¼ yard yellow print for appliqué

¼ yard red print for appliqué

¼ yard green print for sashing

3 yards for backing

ON POINT ALTERNATIVE
INSTRUCTIONS

For an alternative we also made a version with a small green frame and a white border. The blocks are set on point so that the stems of the pomegranates all stand up tall.

The block measurements for both of these four-block quilts are the same. The on point set and border treatments illustrate a typical alternative Catherine and her contemporaries often employed.

Refer to the instructions on page 62 to make the blocks.

* To set blocks on point, from the light muslin, cut
* 1 – 17½" square
* 1 – 25⅜" square. Cut the square from corner to corner twice on the diagonal.

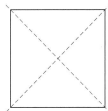

* 2 – 13" squares. Cut the squares from corner to corner once on the diagonal.

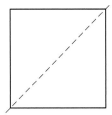

* Sew the rows together on the diagonal adding in the setting triangles and corner triangles. Refer to the setting diagram below if necessary.

BORDERS

* From the green fabric, cut
* 5 – 1¼" strips
* Make two border strips that are 48½" long (or measurement of the quilt from side to side). Sew strips to top and bottom of the quilt.
* Make two border strips that are 50" long (or measurement of the quilt from top to bottom). Sew the strips to either side of the quilt.

* From the background fabric, cut
* 3 – 3½" strips. Make two border strips that are 50" long (or measurement of the quilt from side to side). Sew strips to top and bottom of the quilt.
* 3 – 3½" strips. Make two border strips that are 56" long (or measurement of the quilt from top to bottom). Sew the strips to either side of the quilt.

* Square up the top, if needed. Layer top, batting, backing, baste, quilt and bind.

Quilt Size: 55½" Square • Block Size: 17" Finished
Quilt made by Kathy Moore and quilted by Piecemakers of Lincoln, Nebraska
(with special thanks to Gay Gallup)

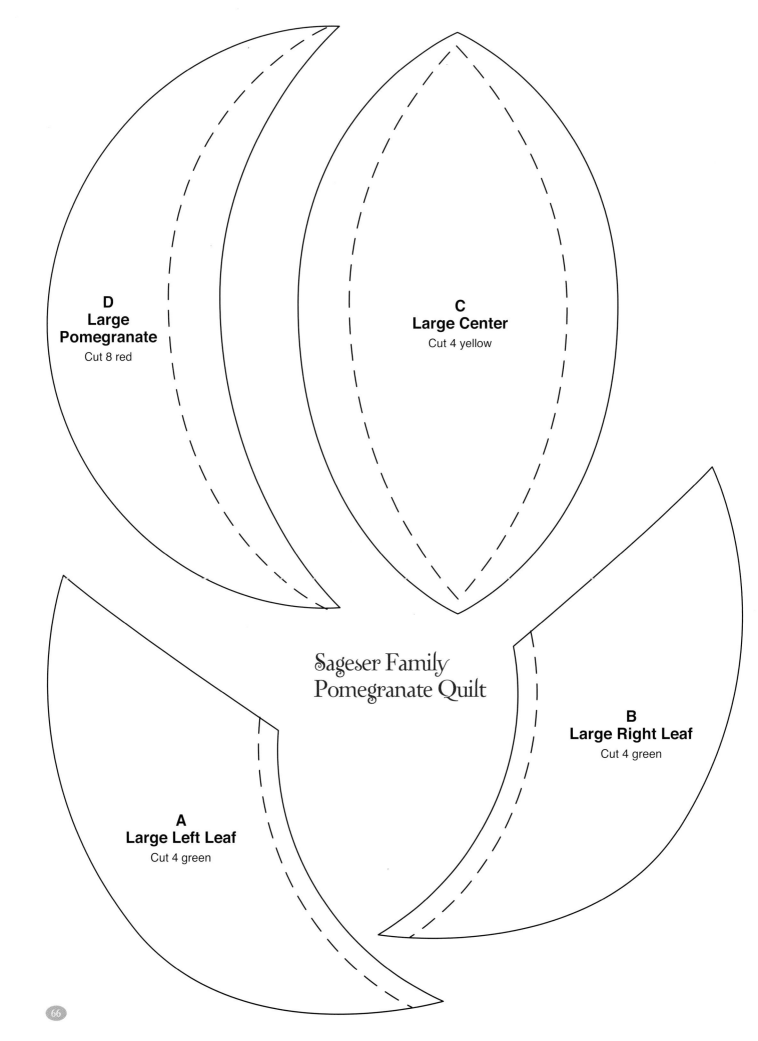

D
Large
Pomegranate

Cut 8 red

C
Large Center

Cut 4 yellow

Sageser Family
Pomegranate Quilt

B
Large Right Leaf

Cut 4 green

A
Large Left Leaf

Cut 4 green

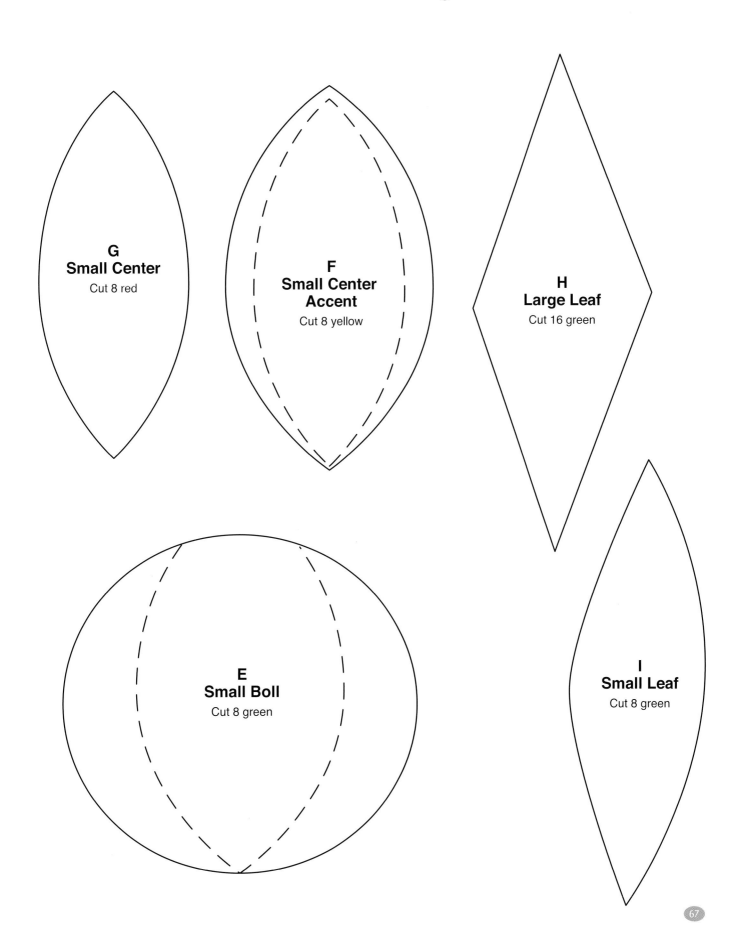

**G
Small Center**

Cut 8 red

**F
Small Center
Accent**

Cut 8 yellow

**H
Large Leaf**

Cut 16 green

**E
Small Boll**

Cut 8 green

**I
Small Leaf**

Cut 8 green

Sageser Family Pots of Tulips Quilt

Donor files at the Nebraska History Museum indicate that Susanette Eby made this lovely quilt entirely by hand in 1847. It reportedly was passed down in her family through her daughter Catherine Eby Miller and came from Indiana to a sod house in Nebraska with Susanette's grand-daughter and Catherine's daughter, Elizabeth Miller Segeser in 1886. It has the natural grace typical of the untrained but gifted quilt makers who were so busy making quilts in mid-nineteenth century.

Much like Catherine Eby Miller's "Pomegranate," Susanette's quilt has nine

blocks. Additionally, it has a wide white border and a narrow binding of the blue print fabric used in some of the appliqué leaves and stems. One wonders if she ran out of green or if she was just expressing her individuality. Most intriguing of all, some of the fabrics from Catherine's "Pomegranate" quilt appear in the flowers on Susanette's quilt.

The documentation is confusing and difficult to decipher. The quilts could have been made anytime from the 1840s to the 1880s, but their innovative and somewhat unpolished representations combined with creative and irregular quilting designs suggest a later date more in keeping with the hardworking agrarian class typical of mid-America in the latter half of the nineteenth century.

Appliqué quilts featuring pots of flowers were a popular theme in the middle to late decades of the nineteenth century and a wide variety of versions similar to the "Pomegranate" and the "Pot of Tulips" abound as can be seen in many state documentation project books and historical websites as well as the Quilt Index (www.quiltindex.org), a very comprehensive and ever growing database of thousands of quilts. The International Quilt Study Center and Museum in Lincoln, Nebraska, also has a large database from which to search (www.quiltstudy.org).

As with the Pomegranate quilt, one of our versions features four blocks. This quilt was hand appliquéd and machine pieced. Reproduction fabrics were used throughout, most of them from collections created by fabric designer Jo Morton.

Quilt Size: 46" Square • Block Size: 18" Finished
Quilt made by Kathy Moore and quilted by Rich O'Hare

FABRIC REQUIREMENTS

2½ yards unbleached muslin for background,
  borders and binding

2 fat eighths of 2 different reds for appliqué

2 fat quarters of 2 different greens for appliqué

1 fat eighth yellow for appliqué

2 fat quarters of 2 different blues for appliqué

2 fat quarters of 2 different tans for appliqué

3 yards for backing

Batting – approximately 52" square

INSTRUCTIONS

❋ From the muslin, cut

❋ 4 – 20" squares

APPLIQUÉ CUTTING GUIDE

❋ 4 – blue long tulip stems cut on bias from scraps or fat quarters ⅞" by 11½"

❋ 4 – green long tulip stems cut on bias from scraps or fat quarters ⅞" by 11½"

❋ 4 – blue short straight bud stems cut on bias ⅞" by 4½" (for yellow flower)

❋ 4 – green short straight bud stems cut on bias ⅞" by 4½" (for yellow flower)

❋ 4 – blue curved bud stems cut on bias ⅞" by 5" (for red flower)

❋ 4 – green curved bud stems cut on bias ⅞" by 5" (for red flower)

❋ For leaves, vases and flowers, refer to the templates on page 74 for cutting directions Add ⅛ – ¼" seam allowance to all appliqué pieces.

❋ Refer to the placement diagram below and appliqué the pieces in place using your favorite method.

❋ When you have finished the appliqué work, trim and square up the blocks to 18½".

❋ Sew the blocks together using the setting diagram on page 71.

BORDERS

❋ From the muslin, cut

❋ 2 – 5½" x 36½" strips (or measurement of the quilt from side to side). Sew the strips to the top and bottom of the quilt

❋ 3 – 5½" strips. Make two border strips that are 46½" long (or measurement of the quilt from top to bottom). Sew the strips to either side of the quilt.

❋ Sew the 5½" x 36" strips to the top and bottom of the quilt.

✳ Square up the top, if needed. Layer the top, batting and backing. Baste, quilt and bind.

✳ The beauty of these blocks is that only small amounts of fabric are needed for each appliqué piece and you can mix in a variety of greens, reds, and yellows to create a lively presentation.

✳ Our patterns assume basic piecing, appliqué, and quilting skills. Beginning quilters may refer to the many Kansas City Star books which provide excellent how-to instructions. Additionally, classes offered through local quilt guilds and shops are also an excellent way to learn the basics. You will find the templates on page 74.

FABRIC REQUIREMENTS
POT OF TULIPS MEDALLION
1¾ yards background, borders and binding

1 fat quarter red for serrated border

Assorted red, green, blue, yellow fat quarters for the
   appliqué pieces. Mix it up when you choose the greens
   for stems and leaves for a more lively and original look

Batting – approximately 38" square

INSTRUCTIONS
POT OF TULIPS MEDALLION
A second quilt, a wallhanging, features a medallion
surrounded by a serrated border. It was also hand
appliquéd and hand quilted.

APPLIQUÉ CUTTING GUIDE
* From the background fabric, cut
* 1 – 26½" square

* For leaves, vase and flowers, refer to the templates on
  page 75 for cutting directions.

* Add ⅛" – ¼" seam allowance to all appliqué pieces.
  In addition, cut the following:
* 2 – long green tulip stems cut on bias from scraps or fat
  quarters ⅞" by 12¾"
* 2 – short green straight stems for yellow bud cut on bias
  ⅞" by 5"
* 2 – green curved stems for red bud cut on bias ⅞"
  by 5½"

* Refer to appliqué placement guide on this page and
  appliqué the pieces in place.

* Trim and square up appliqué block to 24½"

SERRATED BORDER
* From the red fabric, cut
* 8 – 4¼" squares. Cut each square twice from corner
  to corner on the diagonal to yield 32 triangles.

* From background fabric, cut
* 7 – 4¼" squares. Cut each square from corner to corner
  twice on the diagonal to yield 28 white triangles.

* Make 28 units of 2 triangles by setting 1 each of the
  red and white triangles beside each other pointing in
  opposite directions and sew them together on one side.

* Sew the units of red/white together in the same manner
  until you have 4 border strips of 8 red triangles and
  7 white triangles.

* Sew strips to sides of medallion left side and right side,
  then top and bottom.

* Cut 2 – 3⅞" white squares. Cut each square once on the
  diagonal and sew a triangle to each of the 4 corners.

OUTER BORDER
* From background fabric, cut
* 2 – 3" by 28½" strips (or measurement of quilt top from side
  to side). Sew the strips to the top and bottom of the quilt.
* 2 – 3" by 33½" strips (or measurement of quilt top from
  top to bottom). Sew the strips to either side of the quilt.
* Square up the top, if needed. Layer top, batting,
  backing, baste, quilt, and bind.

Quilt Size: 30" • Block Size: 21"
Quilt made and quilted by Kathy Moore

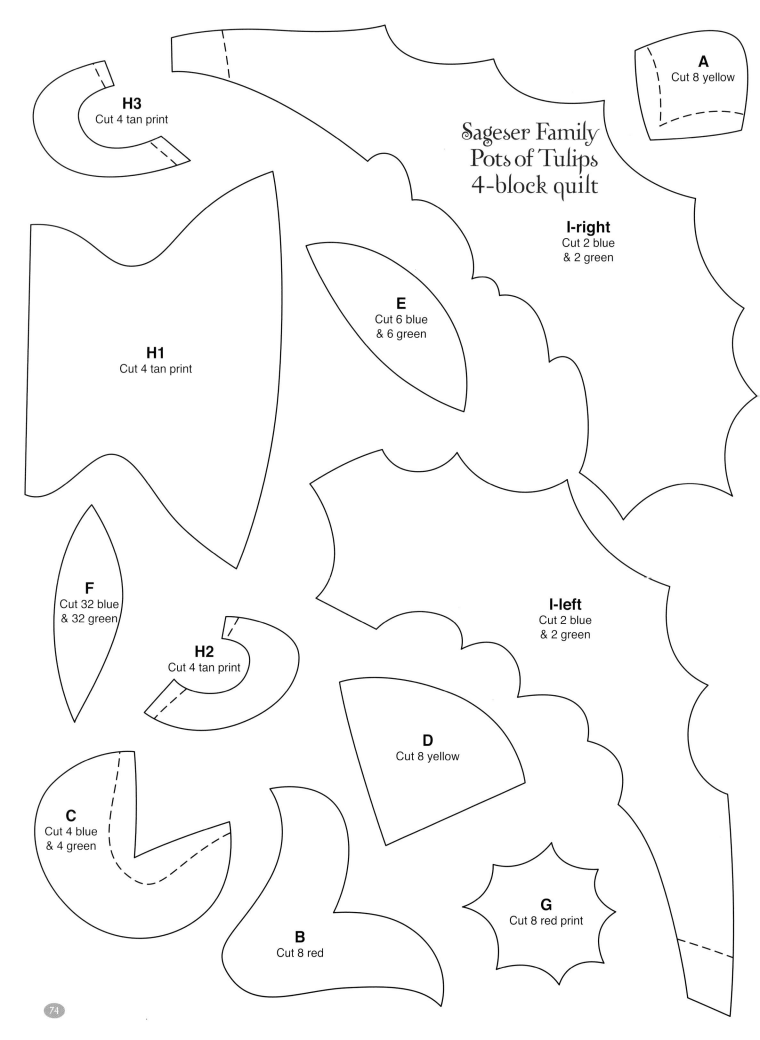

H3
Cut 4 tan print

A
Cut 8 yellow

Sageser Family
Pots of Tulips
4-block quilt

I-right
Cut 2 blue
& 2 green

E
Cut 6 blue
& 6 green

H1
Cut 4 tan print

F
Cut 32 blue
& 32 green

H2
Cut 4 tan print

I-left
Cut 2 blue
& 2 green

D
Cut 8 yellow

C
Cut 4 blue
& 4 green

G
Cut 8 red print

B
Cut 8 red

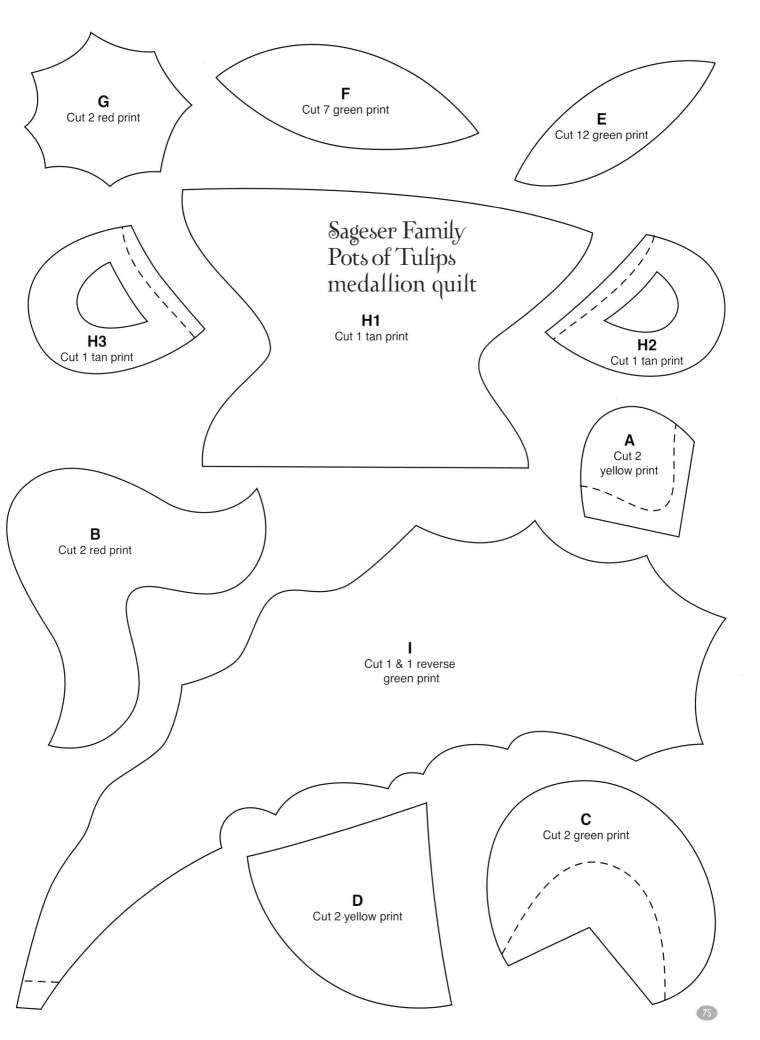

G
Cut 2 red print

F
Cut 7 green print

E
Cut 12 green print

H3
Cut 1 tan print

Sageser Family
Pots of Tulips
medallion quilt

H1
Cut 1 tan print

H2
Cut 1 tan print

A
Cut 2
yellow print

B
Cut 2 red print

I
Cut 1 & 1 reverse
green print

C
Cut 2 green print

D
Cut 2 yellow print

Wood Family Wedge and Circle Quilt

Grace Susannah Budd was born May 10, 1844, at Digby, Nova Scotia, Canada, and was married in February 1875, to James Wood. Shortly thereafter she and James moved to Villisca, Iowa, where they lived for six years before homesteading in Nebraska. Like so many other early immigrants to Nebraska, they lived in a sod house.

Grace's four children were born in Iowa. One died in infancy. Grace Budd Wood died at the age of 71 years and was buried in 1915 at Merna, Nebraska. Her obituary says she lived a life of "earnest toil and loving kindness." It is an epitaph that would probably apply to many women of her age and experience.

Several of her quilts have passed through the generations. These quilts document the changing tastes of quiltmakers over the decades of Grace's life. They begin with an unusual pieced quilt made of blocks Barbara Brackman refers to as either "Wedge and Circle" or "Adam's Refuge" (item #3075 in Brackman's *Encyclopedia of Pieced Quilts*). The blocks were clearly made to celebrate her engagement as illustrated by the risqué comments still legible on each block – written and signed by hand with indelible ink.

INSTRUCTIONS
✳ From the muslin, cut
✳ 16 octagons using template C

✳ From the black, cut
✳ 64 wedges using template B

✳ From the toile, cut
✳ 64 corners/fan blades using template A

Note: ¼" seam allowance **is** included in each of the templates. You will find the templates on page 81.

FABRIC REQUIREMENTS
½ yard muslin
2 yards toile for corner pieces and border
2¾ yards backing fabric
50" square batting
NOTE: Additional fabric will be needed if you want to "fussy cut" the fan blade pieces. Take the template when shopping to plan how to get the correct number of "fussy cut" corner pieces out of the yardage featuring the design to be highlighted. The amount of fabric needed will vary widely depending on the scale of the print.

Above: Grace Susannah Budd Wood
Wedge and Circle Quilt

Quilt Size: 44" Finished
Block Size: 9" Finished
Quilt made by Kathy Moore
and Stephanie Whitson
and quilted by Rich O'Hare

TO MAKE EACH BLOCK

✳ Stitch the wedge and fan blade "frame" together using 4 fan blade pieces (A) and 4 wedge pieces (B).

✳ Lightly draw the stitching line on the center octagon ¼" in from the edge.

✳ With right sides together, hand-stitch the octagon in place in the center of the block. Press.

✳ If desired, trace and embroider fleur de lis in the center of octagon.

✳ Square up each block to 9½".

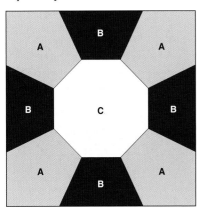

✳ Sew the blocks together into rows of four. Make four rows and stitch together to make the center of the quilt. Refer to the photo on page 77 if necessary.

✳ Measure the quilt through the center from top to bottom. Cut 2 strips from the red piping fabric 1" wide by length of each side.

✳ Fold piping in half and press. Stitch a strip to either side of the quilt using a scant ¼" seam allowance.

✳ Measure the quilt through the center from side to side. Cut 2 strips from the red piping fabric 1" wide by width of the center.

✳ Fold piping in half and press. Stitch a strip to the top and bottom of the quilt using a scant ¼" seam allowance.

BORDERS

✳ From toile fabric, cut

✳ 2 – 4½" x 36½" strips (or measurement of quilt from side to side). Sew strips to top and bottom.

✳ 2 – 4½" x 44½" strips (or measurement of the quilt from top to bottom). Sew strips to the sides.

✳ Layer top, batting, and backing, quilt and bind as desired.

INSTRUCTIONS
ALTERNATE VERSION

Here's another version that adds sashing.
Refer to the directions above and make 9 blocks.

BORDERS AND SASHING

✳ From yellow fabric, cut

✳ 10 – 3" x 9 ¼" sashing strips

✳ 4 – 3" squares

✳ Refer to the diagram on page 80 and sew the sashing strips to the blocks and 3" squares as shown.

✳ From the yellow fabric, cut

✳ 2 – 3" x 32½" strips (or measurement of quilt of side to side). Sew strips to top and bottom

✳ 2 – 3" x 37½" strips (or measurement of the quilt from top to bottom). Sew strips to the sides.

✳ Layer top, batting, and backing, quilt and bind as desired.

FABRIC REQUIREMENTS
ALTERNATE VERSION

⅓ yard muslin
½ yard red
⅔ yard red toile
1 yard yellow for sashing, border and binding
1¼ yards backing fabric
42" square piece batting

Quilt Size: 37" Square • Block Size: 9" Finished
Quilt made and quilted by Stephanie Whitson

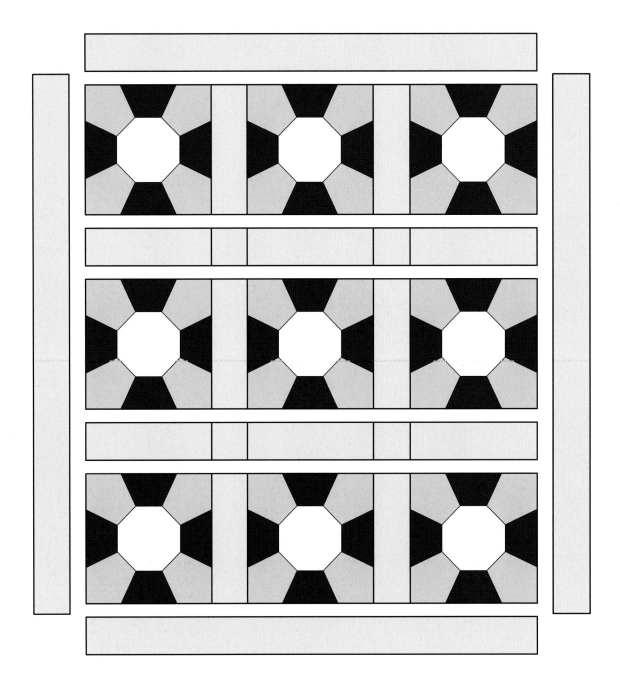

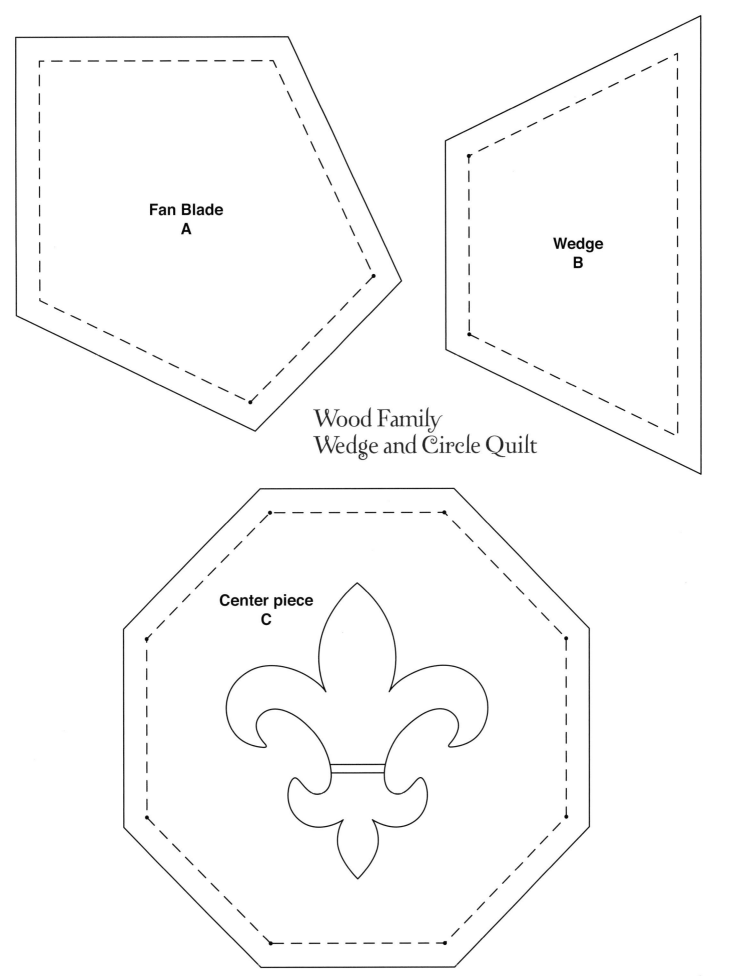

Fan Blade
A

Wedge
B

Wood Family
Wedge and Circle Quilt

Center piece
C

Comer Family Botch Handle Quilt

The unique name for this quilt refers to the forked cast iron tool used to lift the round covers over the burner holes in old cast iron stoves. It's likely that every day many homesteading women used this type of tool while toiling over a hot, and dangerous, wood-burning stove. The photo on page 36 inspired this pattern. Note the quilt on the fence in front of the soddy.

Examples of this quilt block can occasionally be found in antique quilts and are often labeled "Devil's Claw." We prefer the more useful and benign name.

We have seen the pattern done in a variety of fabrics for a scrappy look and in a well-planned and unified choice of colors and fabrics. Done in the quietly elegant style of the Amish, it can have a stunning effect. We chose to make a two-color version and a slightly scrappy version with a dark setting. Both are in keeping with the tastes of the homesteading era.

INSTRUCTIONS

The "Botch Handle" pattern is actually a 9-patch square-in-a-square with star-point sashing.

✳ To make each 9-patch unit, cut
✳ 1 – 2" x 5" strip of dark fabric
✳ 2 – 2" x 5" strips of shirting fabric

✳ Sew a shirting strip to either side of the dark strip to create a light-dark-light strip set. Press the seams toward the dark strip and cut into 2" segments.

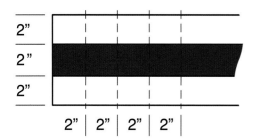

FABRIC REQUIREMENTS FOR BOTCH HANDLE QUILT

Red and White Version
Shown on page 83
¼ yard each of 16 red prints for blocks
¼ yard each of 16 shirting fabrics for blocks
2 yards muslin for sashing, borders and binding
3 yards for backing
1 – 57" square of batting

Scrappy Version
Shown on page 85
¼ yard each of 12 dark fabrics for blocks
¼ yard each of 12 shirting fabrics for blocks
1⅞ yards dark fabric for setting squares, triangles, corners and binding
1½ yards backing
52" x 40" batting

Quilt Size: 5I Square" • Block Size: 8³⁄₈" Finished
Quilt made by Kathy Moore
and quilted by Piecemakers and Friday Afternoon Quilters of Lincoln, Nebraska

✳ Cut: 1 – 2" x 5" strip from dark print.

✳ Sew the 2 pieced strip sets to either side of the dark strip to make a modified 9-patch block. Press seams to the dark strip.

✳ Using the 9-patch for the center, make the square-in-a-square as follows:

✳ Cut 2 – 3½" dark squares. Cut each square from corner to corner once on the diagonal to make corner triangles. Mark the center of each triangle with a tic mark or by folding.

✳ Attach the corner triangles to the 9-patch in this manner:

✳ Mark the center of each side of the 9-patch; match the centers of the triangles to the center of the 9-patch sides and pin; sew one side at a time doing opposite sides in pairs rather than going around clockwise or counter-clockwise.

✳ Press and square up the resulting block at 6⅞".

✳ Make and add the star-point strips

CUTTING INSTRUCTIONS

✳ From the shirting fabric, cut

✳ 4 – 1½" squares for corners

✳ 4 – 1½" x 2⅞" rectangles for spacer strips

✳ 8 – 1½" x 2½" rectangle for flying geese

✳ From the dark fabric, cut

✳ 16 – 1½" squares for flying geese star points

SEWING INSTRUCTIONS

Make 8 flying geese units for the star points.

✳ Draw a line from corner to corner on the reverse side of the dark 1½" squares. Place a dark square atop a 1½" x 2½" shirting rectangle. Stitch along the drawn line. Trim the seam to ¼" and press toward the dark. Repeat on the other side to make a flying geese unit.

✳ Once you have the 8 flying geese made, sew a flying geese unit to either end of a "spacer" strip. Make 2. Sew these to opposite sides of the center square.

✳ Repeat the previous step but add a light corner block at each end. Make 2. Sew each strip to the remaining opposite sides to complete the block.

✳ Press and square up the block to 8⅞".

Quilt Size: 25" x 33" • Block Size: 8¼" Finished
Quilt made by Stephanie Whitson and quilted by Piecemakers and Friday Afternoon
Quilters of Lincoln, Nebraska

TO MAKE THE QUILT

Make 16 Botch Handle blocks

✳ From muslin, cut

✳ 12 – 4" x 8⅞" strips for vertical sashing

✳ 4 – 4" strips. Piece the strips to make 3 horizontal sashing strips 44½" long

✳ Sew 4 blocks and 3 vertical sashes together to make a row. Make 4 rows.

✳ Sew the 3 horizontal sashing strips between the 4 rows of blocks. Refer to the setting diagram below if necessary. Be careful to align the block horizontally and vertically.

BORDER

✳ From the muslin fabric, cut

✳ 5 – 4" strips. Make two border strips that are 44½" long (or measurement of the quilt from side to side). Sew strips to top and bottom of the quilt.

✳ Make two border strips that are 51½" long (or measurement of the quilt from top to bottom). Sew the strips to either side of the quilt.

TO MAKE THE SCRAPPY VERSION

Make 12 Botch Handle blocks

✳ From the dark blue fabric, cut

✳ 6 – 8⅞" squares for setting squares

✳ 3 – 14" squares. Cut each square from corner to corner twice on the diagonal for side setting triangles. There will be 2 unused triangles.

✳ 2 – 7¼" squares. Cut each square from corner to corner once on the diagonal for corner setting triangles

✳ Arrange into diagonal rows using 3 setting triangles on each side and 2 setting triangles on the top and bottom. Add a corner setting triangle at each corner of the quilt. Refer to the setting diagram below and stitch the top together.

✳ Layer the quilt with back and batting. Quilt and bind.

Hersh Family Double 9-Patch Quilt

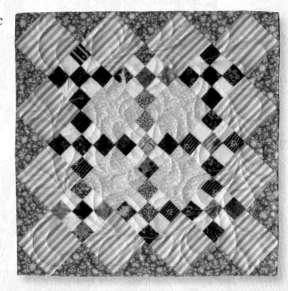

The *Nine-Patch* quilt is a tried and true favorite and is ideal for beginners. When you double the setting you increase the opportunities for interesting interplays between colors, textures, print scales and movement. Our foremothers could use up a lot of little scraps and had endless hours of easy piecing and setting for these blocks, even as they pieced in the poor light of a sod house.

This *Double Nine-Patch* quilt was originally constructed of small fabric scraps in a variety of blues, browns, golds and pinks set with white muslin. The maker, Margaret Alice (Osborn) Raney, was obviously skilled at piecing. Some of the very small squares are even made up of two smaller pieces stitched together to get the 1¼" square.

Margaret Osborn was born in Tennessee in May 1808. She married George Raney in Indiana in February of 1827, and the quilt was made during the first year of her marriage. Upon her death in 1877, her daughter, Mary Jane, inherited the quilt. It subsequently passed through her grandson to a great-granddaughter and namesake, Margaret Alice Hersh, on the occasion of her marriage to Lilburn Oxford in 1903. During the years it was in the possession of her grandson, it was used in a sod house in Custer County.

We like this pretty and cheerful quilt seen on page 43 so much that we attempted to reproduce the quilt as closely as possible using contemporary and reproduction print cotton fabrics. We used a few of our own small scraps and parts of fat quarters purchased to match the original fabrics. We even used one batik because of its resemblance to the original fabric.

When we first viewed Granny Raney's original quilt, our initial thought was "scrappy nine patch strip set—easy." However, the more we studied the quilt, the more impressed we were by her sense of color and balance. The small 9-patches she made incorporated tan, brown, double pink, gold and blue in a multitude of calicos, plaids, and stripes as well as in a variety of dark/medium/light tones. She was obviously working with a very deep scrap bag, but it seems she was *thinking* about balance as she created each 9-patch block.

We came to understand that strip-piecing these nine patches would not yield the desired result. While we have not created a precise roadmap for your scrappy nine-patches, we *have* directed you to acquire a large variety of fabrics. We suggest that you lay each 9-patch out on a design board as you work to achieve balance.

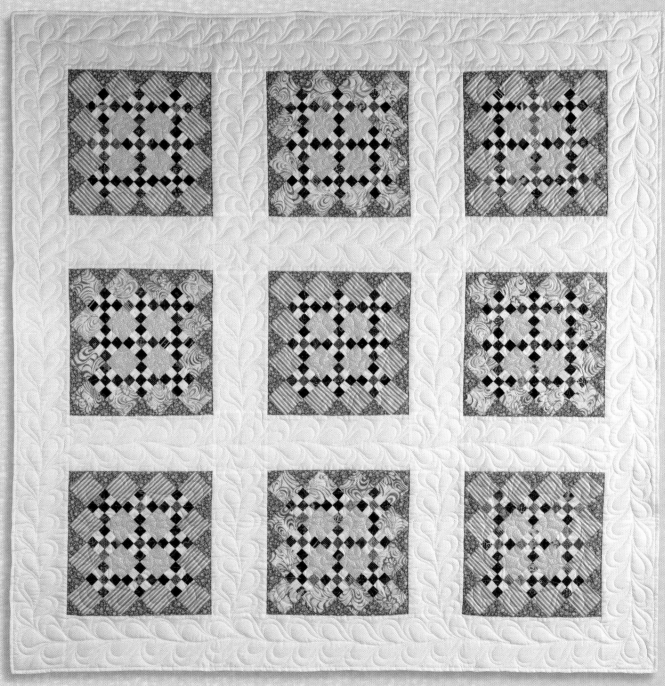

Quilt Size: 57" Square • Block Size: 12½" Finished
Quilt made by Kathy Moore and quilted by Rich O'Hare

FABRIC REQUIREMENTS

3 fat eighths light blue prints

3 fat eighths light double pink prints

3 fat eighths light tan or gold prints

1 fat eighth light tan or gold plaid or stripe.

3 fat eighths medium blue prints.

3 fat eighths medium pink prints

3 fat eighths medium tan plaid

3 fat eighths dark blue print

3 fat eighths dark brown print

3 fat eighths dark gold stripe or plaid

1 fat eighth dark tan plaid or stripe.

⅓ yard aqua/white print for center squares

½ yard blue/white stripe for outer edge squares
of 5 blocks

⅜ yard batik for outer edge squares of 4 blocks

1¼ yard tan print for border triangles

2¼ yard light muslin for 9-patch blocks, sashing, border,
and binding

3½ yards for backing

Batting – approximately 62" square

INSTRUCTIONS

❋ For each small 9-patch block, cut

❋ 5 – 1¼" squares from assorted fat eighths. Each block
should incorporate light, dark and medium tones.

❋ 4 – 1¼" squares light muslin

❋ Sew the squares together into rows of 3. Sew 3 rows
together to make a 9-patch unit. Refer to the diagram
below. Make 81.

❋ Press and trim each 9-patch block to measure
2¾" square.

❋ For setting squares to fit beside the small 9-patch blocks

❋ From the aqua/white print, cut

❋ 36 – 2¾" squares for center setting squares

❋ From the blue/white stripe, cut

❋ 60 – 2¾" squares for outer edge setting squares for 5
blocks

❋ From the batik, cut

❋ 48 – 3¾" squares for outer edge setting squares for 4
blocks

❋ From the tan print, cut

❋ 27 – 5¼" squares. Cut each square from corner to
corner twice on the diagonal to make 108 side setting
triangles

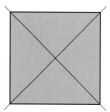

❋ 18 – 3" squares. Cut each square from corner to corner
once on the diagonal to make 36 corner triangles

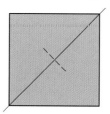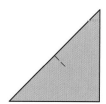

❋ Refer to the diagram for the arrangement of 9-patch
blocks, side and corner triangles

❋ Sew diagonal sets of blocks and triangles into strips as
shown below.

* Add the corner triangles last by matching the centers of triangles to the centers of unfinished corners.

* Make 9 blocks.

* Press and square up the blocks to 13 inches.

SASHING AND BORDERS
* From the light muslin, cut
* 4 – 5¼" squares for cornerstones
* 12 – 5¼" x 13" strips for sashing

* Sew 2 sashes between 3 blocks to make a row. Make 3 rows. Sew 2 cornerstones between 3 sashes. Make 2 of these rows. Refer to the diagram and sew the rows of blocks and sashing together.

* From the light muslin, cut
* 6 – 5 ¼" strips. Make two border strips that are 47 ½" long (or measurement of the quilt from side to side). Sew strips to top and bottom of the quilt.

* Make two border strips that are 57" long (or measurement of the quilt from top to bottom). Sew the strips to either side of the quilt.

* Square up the top, if needed. Layer top, batting, backing, baste, quilt, and bind.

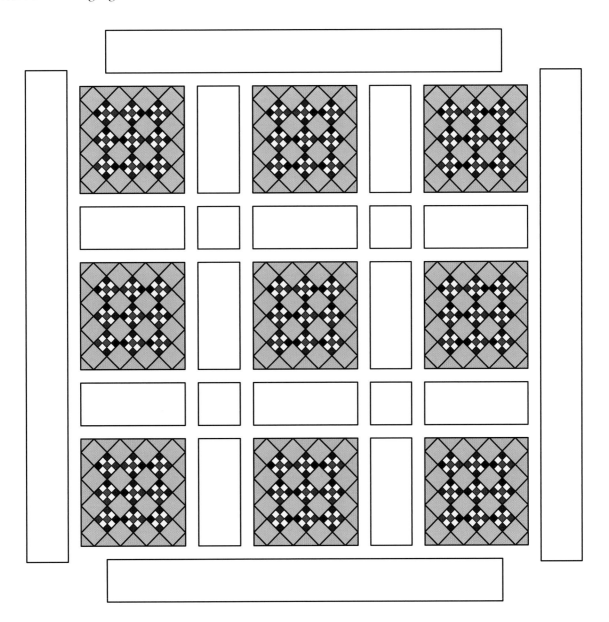

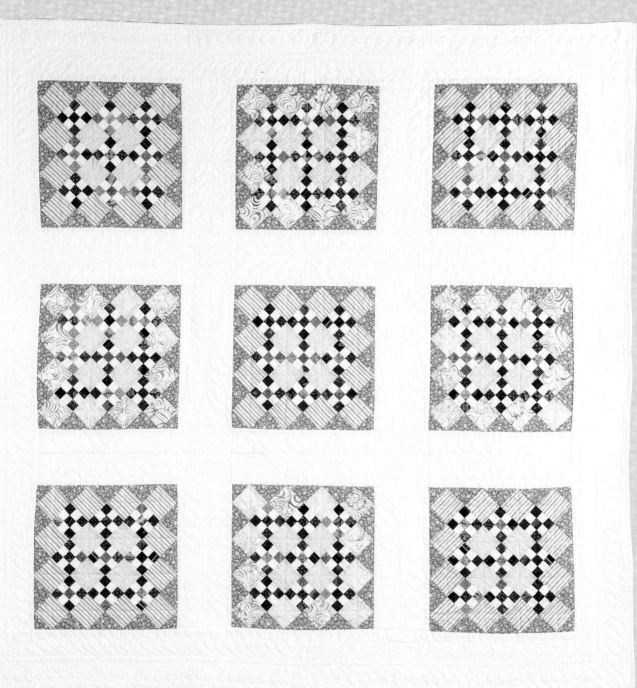

Quilt Size: 57" • Block Size: 12½" finished
Quilt made by Stephanie Whitson,
hand quilted by Piecemakers and Friday Afternoon Quilters of Lincoln, Nebraska

PART ONE – ARRIVING

[1]Mrs. Jim Klepper, "Memories of Pioneer Days," undated, in May Avery papers, Nebraska State Historical Society, Lincoln (NSHS).

[2]G.R. McKeith, *Pioneer Stories of the Pioneers of Fillmore and Adjoining Counties,* (Exeter, NE: Press of Fillmore County News, 1915).

[3] Klepper, "Memories…"

[4] Everett Dick, *The Sod-House Frontier 1854-1890* (Lincoln, NE: Johnsen Publishing Company, 1954).

[5]Homer Socolofsky, "The Homestead Story," *Nebraska History Magazine,* Autumn, 1967.

[6]Mabel Randel Vernon, "The Life and Works of Mabel Randel Vernon," Nebraska State Historical Society, Lincoln (NSHS).

[7]Mrs. William McGhies of Aberdeen, Scotland, quoted in response to her husband's musings about returning home, in McKeith, Pioneer Stories … .

[8]Harry L. Crawford Papers, "*Notes and Dates from Diary of Mrs. Emily Carpenter*," Nebraska State Historical Society, Lincoln (NSHS).

[9]Frederick C. Luebke, *Nebraska, An Illustrated History* (Lincoln, NE: University of Nebraska Press, 1995).

[10]Everett Dick, *Sod-House Frontier.*

[11]Luna Sanford Kellie, Nebraska State Historical Society, Lincoln (NSHS).

[12]Susan Carter Payne, Nebraska State Historical Archive, Lincoln (NSHS).

[13]In his history of the Loup Valley, near where Susan lived and taught, H. W. Foght discusses general meetings and decisions within the community of Lee's Park, Joint District No. 11 of Custer and Valley counties, to build a sod school house during the fall of 1878. A sod school was completed the follow fall and he notes that it was used for many years until it was declared unsafe…" H. W. Foght, *Trail of the Loup Being a History of the Loup River Region with Some Chapters on the State,* (Ord, NE: 1906), 154-155.

[14]Celia Y. Oliver, *Enduring Grace: Quilts from the Shelburne Museum Collection* (Lafayette, CA: C&T Publishing, 1997), 34. Oliver cites Linda Otto Lipsett, *Pieced from Ellen's Quilt* (Ohio: Halstead and Meadows Publishing, 1991), 201. Lippsett's book contains extensive quotations from the diary of Ellen Spaulding Reed, a woman who moved west with her husband from Vermont to Wisconsin in the middle third of the 19th century. She is quoted a number of times referring to the piecing of comfortables, one of which she gave the name "Bonaparts retreat." Ellice Ronsheim writes in the book she co-authored with Ricky Clark and George W. Knepper, *Quilts In Community: Ohio's Traditions,* that comforts or comforters were coarsely-made quilts that could be pieced of blocks or strips of cloth and thickly filled with batting; tied or coarsely quilted, and that they would provide years of practicable service, be easy to clean if tied rather than quilted and could be covered by a more decorative spread if desired. She quotes a number of published articles and probate records but notes that the Ohio documentation project found few of these quilts. She assumes they were used up and discarded or thought not worthy of documentation by the owners of any surviving quilts. Barbara Brackman, in her book, *Clues in the Calico,* specifies that comforters are mentioned in a few estate inventories, diaries, and letters in the 1840s and 1850, but that surviving examples commonly date from 1875 to the 1940s. She describes them as crudely and quickly made with strips of fabric yardage or simply pieced of calico or of wool—made by rural women for warm bedding. No time or materials were wasted in their construction. They were usually tied to hold the layers together.

[15]Photocopy of Will Payne's obituary sent to K. Moore by Becci Thomas, Director, Knight Museum & Sallows Military Museum, Alliance, NE.

[16]From the epilogue to Susan Carter Payne's 1887 diary, MS0846, Nebraska State Historical Archive, Lincoln (NSHS).

[17]Photocopy of Will Payne's obituary.

[18]Luna Kellie (NSHS).

[19]Leo L. Lemonds., D.V.M., *Letters from Nebraska Sod House Pioneers* (Hastings, NE: Cornhusker Press, 2004).

PART TWO – SETTLING IN

[1]Katie Goar Maze, *Looking Backward* (Harrisburg, The Evangelical Press, 1943).

[2]Mattie Oblinger letter of March 25, 1878.

[3]Mattie Oblinger letter of September 20, 1878.

[4]Uriah Oblinger to Mattie Oblinger, February 9, 1873, Nebraska State Historical Society.

[5] J.W. Kaura, *Saline County Nebraska History Beginning in 1858* (Nebraska Farmer Co., Lincoln, NE), 166.

[6]Uriah Oblinger to Mattie Oblinger, April 13, 1873, Nebraska State Historical Society (NSHS).

[7]Uriah Oblinger to Mattie Oblinger, April 13, 1873, Nebraska State Historical Society (NSHS).

[8]Mattie Oblinger letter of June 16, 1873, Nebraska State Historical Society (NSHS).

[9]Luna Kellie (NSHS).

[10]Grace Snyder, *No Time on My Hands* (The Caxton Printer, Ltd., Caldwell, ID, c. 1963), 320-321.

[11] Katie Goar Maze, ...*Backward,* 50-51.

[12] Mrs. Thompson Lamphere, "Buck and Berry Were Water Boys," *Cradle Days in York County* (York, NE: the *York Republican*, November, 1937).

[13] Mattie Oblinger, letter home, June 16, 1873.

[14]Ibid.

[15]Katie Goar Maze, ...*Backward.*

[16]From the original letters of Julia Baptist, Nebraska State Historical Society (NSHS) MS408.

[17]Lizzie Wirt, "The Faith Nothing Could Defeat," *Cradle Days in York County* (York, NE: the *York Republican*, November, 1937), 53.

[18]Mrs. H.J. Yeck, "A Snake Was Her Bedfellow," *Anecdotes of Custer County, Nebraska* (Broken Bow, NE: The *Custer County Chief*), 36.

[19]Mattie Oblinger letter of August 25, 1874.

[20]Esther Imel Bailey, "Levi Imel Family Joins the Pioneers," *Cradle Days in York County* (York, NE: the *York Republican*, November, 1937), 104.

[21]Maggie Oblinger Sandon, recollections, Uriah Oblinger papers, Nebraska State Historical Society (NSHS).

[22]Ibid.

[23] Cora Ellis Austin, "Early Comers on Tinker's Ridge," *Cradle Days in York County* (York, Nebraska: the *York Republican*, November, 1937), 57.

[24]Snyder, *No Time On My Hands.*

PART THREE – STAYING ON

[1]McGhies in McKeith, *Pioneer Stories* ... .

[2]S.A. Myers, "Experiences of a Cradle Rocker," *Cradle Days in York County* (York, NE: the *York Republican,* November, 1937), 79.

[3]Katie Goar Maze, ...*Backward,* 55.

[4]Ibid., p. 69.

[5]Charles S. Reed, "Life in a Nebraska Soddy: A Reminiscence," *Nebraska History Magazine,* March (1958): 57-73.

[6]Lizzie Lockwood, *American Life Histories: Manuscripts from the Federal Writers' Project,* www.loc.gov.

[7]Reed.

[8]Mattie V. Oblinger letter to Thomas Family, April 12, 1874.

[9]Mrs. George Johnson Kelley in Bayard H. Paine, *Pioneers, Indians and Buffaloes* (Curtis, NE: The Curtis Enterprise, 1935).

[10]Mrs. Ina M. Abrahamzon in *Sod House Pioneering,* Nebraska State Historical Society (NSHS).

[11]Charles Henry Morrill, quoted in "Sunbonnet and Calico," *Nebraska History Magazine,* March (1966).

[12]W.A. Stevens, *Sod House to Shelterbelt, A Pioneer Story* (Palmer, NE The Palmer Journal, 1951).

[13]Abrahamzon.

[14]Mrs. Emily Carpenter, "Notes and Dates from Diary of Mrs. Emily Carpenter, Nebraska State Historical Society (NSHS).

[15]Private family papers belonging to descendents of Mrs. Wood.

Acknowledgments

We began researching sod house quilts over five years ago. A project that lasts that long inevitably benefits from the input, expertise, and wisdom of dozens of people, not to mention the unending patience of husbands. We owe a special debt to our husbands, Ray Moore and Dan Higgins, for believing in us and being willing to endure.

Thank you, Kansas City Star Books. Diane McClendon and Doug Weaver, your "yes" and your enthusiasm for this project made a dream come true. Aaron Leimkuhler, photo day was a delight. Amy Robertson, Eric Sears, and Jane Miller, thank you for taking our fuzzy vision and not only giving it clarity, but making it more beautiful than we hoped. Editor Extraordinaire Edie McGinnis…you deserve a halo. Thank you for putting up with two first-time authors who didn't know how much they didn't know.

WE ALSO WISH TO THANK:
The Nebraska State Historical Society
Especially Deb Arenz, Linda Hein, Mary Jo Miller, and John Carter for their unflagging enthusiasm, support, and ever-patient answers to endless questions
The Custer County Historical Society
Especially Mrs. Mary Landkamer (who knows everything, and shares her knowledge willingly), and other wonderful volunteers including Mr. Don Davis.
The International Quilt Study Center and Museum
Especially Director Dr. Patricia Cox Crews and Collections Manager Janet Price.

Quilt owners and descendents of pioneers who shared family stories, cherished artifacts, and quilts.
Mrs. and Mrs. Eugene Burkhead
Mrs. Marge Caldwell
Mr. and Mrs. Dan Hersh
Dr. and Mrs. Leo Lemonds
Mrs. Ellen Lessman
Custer County residents and pioneer descendents Althea Ferguson and Em and Ron Jorgenson whose guided tours of back roads and Custer County soddies was unforgettable.
Piecemakers Quilt Group of the University of Nebraska Women's Club.
Mary Burrow, Joanna Fink, Linda Gosey, Judy Hendrix, Gail Keown, Nancy Klopfenstein, Kaye Miller, Wanda Omtvedt, Rogene Silletto, Dottie Wolverton, Erny Von Bargen and especially Gaye Gallup, who helped us meet our deadlines with unswerving support and who donated a very fast needle both to quilting and bindings.
Friday Afternoon Quilters, Carol Christensen, Carol Curtis, Imagean Lind, Genie Sullivan, Ginny Welty.
Jo Morton, quilt designer extraordinaire and friend, for inspiration, insight, and support.
Janet Barber, quilt maker, and friend, for proof-reading our instructions and making us laugh (errors are OURS, not hers).
Brooke Reinhard, daughter and friend, for staging things so beautifully for photography.
Rich and Roxanne O'Hare of The Cosmic Cow in Lincoln, Nebraska, for advice and amazing long-arm quilting.
And Chester, who tolerated a stranger invading his home with mostly good grace, and never failed to remind us when it was time for a snack.

About the Authors

KATHY MOORE

Kathleen L. (Kathy) Moore lives in Lincoln, Nebraska, where she divides her time volunteering at the International Quilt Study Center and Museum (IQSC/M), researching Nebraska history, making quilts, quilting with friends as often as possible and wrangling her husband, Ray, and two cats, Chester and Jessicat. She also has two beloved daughters and three beautiful grandchildren.

Already an accomplished dressmaker, Moore began quilting in her 40s while living in Lawrence, KS. Her first quiltmaking class required her to hand piece and appliqué a small sample quilt. She finished the piece, thinking all the while that a sewing machine would make the project go faster. Many quilts and a few years later, Moore and her husband moved to Lincoln, Nebraska.

When a friend of a friend invited her to help vacuum and fold quilts for storage at the newly created IQSC, a new aspect of quilting opened itself to her and soon she was working on a second master's degree, this time in textile history with an emphasis in quilt studies.

Moore is a current member of the Lincoln (NE) Quilters Guild and the Nebraska State Quilt Guild; a board member of the American Quilt Study Group; a member of the American Quilter's Society; the Nebraska Statue Historical Society; and a friend and volunteer at the IQSC/M; and a member of the Textile Society of America.

STEPHANIE GRACE WHITSON

Stephanie Grace Whitson is a full time novelist/lecturer, an incurable quilt enthusiast, a student working on her Master's degree in history, a grandmother, and a biker who enjoys motorcycle trips with her blended family and church friends. She began quilting in earnest as a young mother. Soon thereafter, she co-founded Mulberry Lane, a quilt pattern design company that also marketed sewing related pewter jewelry to quilt shops. She has been an antique quilt and sewing tools dealer, has taken several quilt appraisal/textile dating classes, and volunteers at the International Quilt Study Center and Museum. Offered a publishing contract for her first historical novel in 1994, Stephanie has published sixteen historical novels, three contemporary novels, two works of non-fiction, and recently signed a contract for a series of quilt-related historical novels. She is a frequent lecturer/guest speaker/workshop leader for various church and civic organizations including quilt guilds. Visit her at www.stephaniewhitson.com or www.footnotesfromhistory.blogspot.com.